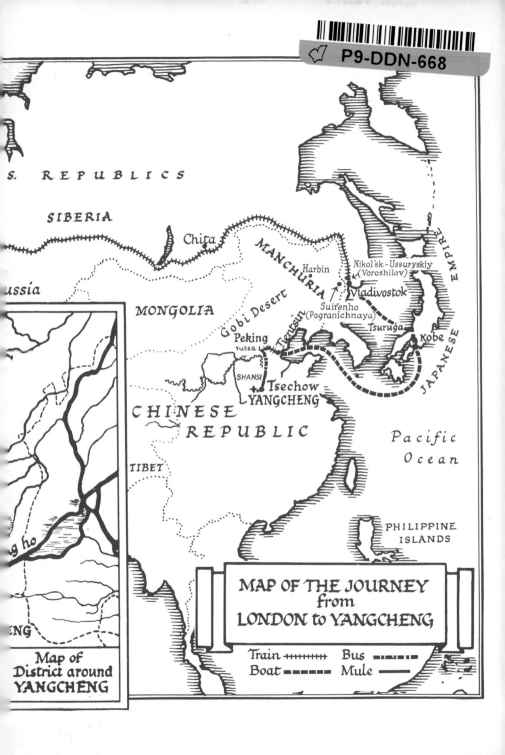

S. REPUBLICS

SIBERIA

Chita

MANCHURIA

Harbin

Nikol'sk - Ussuryskiy
(Voroshilov)

ussia

MONGOLIA

Gobi Desert

Vladivostok

Suifenho
(Pogranichnaya)

Tsuruga

Peking

Tientsin

Kobe

JAPANESE EMPIRE

Tutsa

SHANSI

Tsechow
YANGCHENG

CHINESE
REPUBLIC

Pacific
Ocean

TIBET

PHILIPPINE
ISLANDS

ng ho

MAP OF THE JOURNEY
from
LONDON to YANGCHENG

ENG

Map of
District around
YANGCHENG

Train ++++++++   Bus ━ ━ ━
Boat ------   Mule ━━━

The

Small

Woman

To dear Marian –
for her June '72 graduation.
Blessings –
    Miriam

The

Small

Woman

by Alan Burgess

WITH ILLUSTRATIONS AND MAPS

E. P. DUTTON & CO., INC.
NEW YORK

Library of Congress Catalog Card Number: 57–7603
Montauk Book Manufacturing Company, Inc., New York

ILLUSTRATIONS
Photographs

Illustrations

The

Small

Woman

CHAPTER ONE

THE WHOLE AFFAIR of the small woman both intrigued and concerned the Senior Physician. That she was dying he did not doubt. Who she was, no one knew. But in China, in those autumn days of 1941, with the Japanese invader pressing in on many fronts and one half of the world trying hard to destroy the other in a furious holocaust of tanks and planes, guns and ships, violent death was such a near neighbor that the departure from this life of one small, unknown woman was of little concern to anyone.

The few English-speaking staff members of the Scandinavian-American Mission at the town of Hsing P'ing, deep in beleaguered northwest China, knew neither her name nor where she came from. Two Chinese peasants had delivered her to the front gate. They had admitted to the gateman that if she had been Chinese they would have left her to die. They knew she was a foreigner, even though she was dressed in Chinese clothes and carried a Chinese Bible; therefore they thought it more seemly that she should die close to her friends, her soul consigned to her own gods. Then the peasants retreated into the unknown, and the gateman went to tell his masters that they had a dying woman on their hands.

The Scandinavian-American Mission wired at once to the Baptist Mission Hospital at Sian, asking if a doctor could come; and with a generous humanity which in the next few weeks was to be freely given by all at that hospital, the

Senior Physician came the same day by train. He arrived late that afternoon, and examined the patient. She must be about thirty-five, he thought. Her body was thin and under-nourished; crow's feet of weariness and suffering ran in dark lines from the corners of her eyes; she bore the scar of a fairly recent bullet wound across her back; and although it was not apparent, she was also suffering from internal in-juries, caused by a brutal beating which had taken place some months earlier.

Her temperature was 105 degrees; she was in a raving de-lirium, and she was quite certain that the Senior Physician was a Japanese officer.

His long experience in the Northwest told him that she was probably suffering from relapsing fever. He took an im-mediate blood slide, and sent it back by special messenger to the Baptist Hospital. A second messenger returned next day with news that the blood film confirmed that he had diag-nosed correctly. At once he gave her an intravenous injection which he knew would lessen the fever. As by this time a Swedish-American nurse named Miss Nelson had also ar-rived, he felt that he could now leave the patient in her hands, for the fever would abate within forty-eight hours, and only time and good nursing could effect a cure. He re-turned to Sian, content that he had done all he could.

Five days later, a telegram to the Baptist Hospital in-formed the Senior Physician that the unknown woman was again in a violent delirium. Although her temperature had, indeed, dropped to near normal, it had suddenly shot up again to 105 degrees, and she was dangerously ill.

He caught the next train and found his patient just break-ing out in the rash of that most deadly disease, typhus, which she must have been incubating while suffering from relaps-ing fever! As three doctors at the Baptist Hospital had died of typhus during the past few years, and as the resistance of this woman, because of malnutrition, shock, and fatigue, was negligible, in his own mind the Senior Physician held out no hope for her at all. Especially when further examination revealed that a patch of pneumonia had developed on one lung.

By a God-given coincidence, however, one of the Hsing P'ing missionaries, who had just returned from furlough in the United States, had about twenty tablets of the new drug, sulfapyridine, in his personal kit. These he gladly offered to the Senior Physician as treatment for the woman. Using this antibiotic, the Baptist doctor managed to curb the pneumonia; but it was clear to him that if the small woman was to have the slightest chance of survival, she would have to be moved to the hospital at Sian at once.

The Senior Physician had been in China for nearly twenty years. He had survived the siege of Sian when the armies of two local warlords had fought for the city and twenty thousand people had died of starvation. He had many contacts and some influence in the district, and for this small, unknown woman he did not hesitate to use both. By good luck he succeeded in reaching by phone a friend of his who managed that section of the railroad. Addressing him by his nickname, he said:

"Rails? I want a special car attached to the first train that leaves tomorrow. We've a patient we shall carry to the train on a camp bed, and we shall have four helpers to hold it steady during the journey. Will you do this for me? It's urgent!"

Rails said he would. Had the small woman, in her delirium, known that a private car was being arranged for her benefit alone, she would certainly have laughed until she cried.

11

The train was met at Sian by bearers, and the unconscious woman was taken to the hospital. One of the lady doctors cheerfully gave up her room so that the desperately sick woman could have the benefit of a large and airy chamber. Miss Nelson and the hospital matron, Miss Major, continued to nurse her.

It was fifteen days later, when the typhus fever was beginning to abate, that the Japanese, after several weeks of inactivity, decided that they would bomb Sian. The Senior Physician sat with his patient as the bombs began to fall. He still knew nothing of her history, for during the two weeks she had been in Sian, the fever had never left her mind clear. Now her thin, wasted form jerked and twitched in agony as each bomb whistled down, and the rumble and crash shook the room. Her whole body ran with a cold sweat, as she struggled to rise, and the doctor, who in all his experience had never seen such an agony of delayed shock, held her wrists and tried to comfort her.

"My children," she gasped. "Where are my children? The Japanese are bombing us. . . ."

The Senior Physician tried to calm her. At last the bombers' undertone receded, the all-clear siren wailed distantly, the small woman's tense muscles relaxed. Her fever had seemed to be subsiding, but the raid had had an unusually bad effect on her. He felt that he must find out something about her.

She was still almost a complete enigma. As Miss Nelson stood by her next day, a spasm of pain crossed her face and a whisper came from her lips. "Not much farther now, children." Then suddenly she was talking in a Chinese dialect which no one could understand at first, but which someone finally recognized as coming from a wild mountain district far to the north. Later that morning a faint smile formed on her face. There was nostalgic reminiscence in the painfully articulated words: "Remember that first night of *Lilac Time?* That little tune?"

From the constricted throat, slowly into the hot room of the hospital, came the short, uncertain notes of a tune every errand boy had been whistling a generation ago. Presently they grew fainter and stopped; the spell of delirium passed, and the patient lay quiet, her eyes closed.

Miss Nelson noiselessly left the room. "She's sleeping quietly at last, poor thing," she told a Chinese nurse in the corridor. "If only the rest will break the fever, and she can tell us who she is and something about herself!"

That afternoon the small woman opened her eyes. She saw the neat, western-style room, the curtains hanging limp in the heat, the whitewashed ceiling where flies buzzed lazily. Flies? There were flies on the faces of the dead at Yangcheng. But where was this? The clean bed, the metal bedside table —she must be in some mission building. And who was that tall man who had bent over her so many times and with such quiet persistence had probed into her past? What did he want? How could she make him—or anyone—understand? It was all simple enough, really, but it would take a long time to tell. She closed her eyes. The thin sheets felt soft and comfortable. She would think back and consider how much she would tell them. It was not unpleasant to lie here in a world of darkness and color, and let one's mind drift back down the years.

They had been good years. No one could take them away from her. For days people had been asking her name. But everyone knew that. Ai-weh-deh, the Virtuous One! Everyone in the province of Shansi knew that. But, of course, you did not always tell your English name.

The night that she'd met General Ley in the mountain village, for instance. He was a Roman Catholic priest, but she never knew his real name; she had only heard vaguely that he was Dutch. He had sat across the table from her, the yellow light from the flickering castor-oil lamp stenciling black shadows into his face. They had talked hour after hour of the immense dilemma in their hearts; then he'd gone away into the darkness, his black robe flapping around his legs, gone back over the mountains with his rifle to rejoin his band of armed guerrillas . . . to kill.

And there were many others she'd known in Shansi. The Mandarin, in his gown of scarlet, sculptured silk, living in his mountain *yamen* among the wild peaks. And Sualan, the pretty one, she with the pale skin and hands as restless and delicate as butterflies, dedicated from birth to be a smiling slave girl to all the Mandarin's retainers; and Feng, the Buddhist priest, shaven-headed, condemned to years in that filthy jail; or the muleteer whose wife and children they burned to death. And Linnan, the man she loved, who had sent scouts looking for her in the mountains. . . .

The gentle voice in her ear had been insistent. "Tell us your name," it had said. "Don't be frightened. There's no need to be frightened now."

Frightened! Being frightened did not concern her any more. She had been frightened sleeping in the snow among those dark Siberian pines; frightened of the man who had trapped her in that hotel bedroom in Vladivostok; frightened in that dreadful Chinese prison when the maniac with the bloodstained ax turned toward her; frightened in the mountain cave when the wolves howled and their eyes were tiny, reflected lights in the darkness; frightened when the Japanese cried "Halt," and the bullets ricocheted from the tombstones all around her. . . .

The Small Woman

It seemed so silly to keep asking her name. Surely they knew her name was Gladys Aylward, and that she had been born in Edmonton. They must have heard of Edmonton, in the north of London. And yet—it was so very far away, so long ago. She would try to see if she could remember. And presently it all came back to her, just as it had been in those days when Edmonton was her entire world, and an omnibus ride to Selfridge's or to a Christmas pantomime in Drury Lane had seemed like a far and adventurous journey.

In those days the fields had flowed right up to the boundaries of Edmonton, but that was before the gray stone, the red brick and the grime of London City had imprisoned the former suburb. They had moved to Cheddington Road when she was very small. A row of red brick houses, lace curtains, privet hedges, Aspidistras in the windows. Gray pavements. Each morning an unending procession of cheerful milkmen, greengrocers, bakers and their horse-drawn carts moving along the streets. A happy childhood! She remembered her father coming home, clumping up the road in his heavy postman's boots, wearing his dark uniform with the red piping. Mum would be in the kitchen getting the tea, and she and Violet would be screaming around the house or running wild with the other children in the street.

When the Zeppelins came over to bomb London in the First World War, she remembered how she'd first discovered the antidote to being "frightened." She would bring all the children in the street into the front parlor and sit them down against the inside wall. Then she would sit at the tiny old foot-operated organ, pedal furiously and scream out a hymn at a decibel scale calculated to reach almost as high as those ominous silver cocoons droning through the sky.

Later, during her years in China, she had discovered again

how singing could lift people's hearts, no matter how depressing the circumstances. Hadn't they sung as they had marched over the mountains, all those tired and footsore children, marching not on Jordan, but down to the immense, untamed, ancient configurations of the Yellow River. And she remembered the disappointment there. Was there ever a disappointment to equal it? Maybe that time in London at the China Inland Mission? Maybe that disappointment would equal it?

It had been after some years of employment as a parlormaid in London that she had tried to take the course at the Mission Center in order to qualify as a China missionary. Even now she remembered the way the black winter branches swayed against the pale London sky outside the Principal's study window. The Principal of the Mission Center, a tall, thin, scholarly man with a domed forehead, had faced her across the table. The edges of his kindly blue eyes were a network of deep, interconnecting lines; bushy gray eyebrows jutted above. She remembered even now how he'd looked at her, oh! so seriously. She had been twenty-six years old, very small and slender, with a neat figure, dark brown eyes, an oval face, and dark hair parted in the middle and gathered at the back into an uncompromising bun. Perhaps the Principal discerned some of the inherent stubbornness and inner strength in the tightening of her lips. But he would also see the tension in her face: tension that would soon be replaced by disappointment.

He had spread the reports in front of him and pursed his lips.

"You've been with us now for three months, I see, Miss Aylward?" he said.

"Yes, sir."

"Theology, now?"

"I wasn't very good at theology, was I?" she had said quietly.

He had looked up under his eyebrows. "No, you weren't. Not good at all!"

She remembered how she sat with her fingers tightly clenched in her lap. She hardly heard the voice which reiterated her list of failures. She knew she could never make him understand. She knew she lacked the persuasiveness to argue with him or the education to pass his examinations; she knew she hadn't the "background"; she knew she had no chance. But she knew also, with a single-minded, agonizing clearness, that she *must* go to China.

"You see, Miss Aylward, all these scholastic shortcomings are important," he had said, sympathetically, "but most important of all is your age. If you had stayed at the China Inland Mission Center for another three years and then we sent you out you would be about thirty by the time you arrived." He had shaken his head doubtfully. "Our experience tells us that students older than thirty, unless they are quite exceptional, find it extremely difficult to learn the Chinese language.

"In view of all this you will understand, I'm sure," he had continued, "that there seems to be little point in your continuing with your studies here at the College. We accepted you to be trained in good faith, on trial. If you went on, it would be a waste of everyone's time and money, and . . ." He left the sentence unfinished.

"I understand," she said quietly. "Thank you for letting me come. It's not your fault that I couldn't do all these things."

The Principal had tried to soften the disappointment. "You mustn't be too distressed at this . . . er . . . setback. There is so much other useful work to be done in Britain

17

by people like yourself." He had paused. "Have you any idea what you will do now?"

"No," she said.

He glanced at her papers. "I see you were in . . . er . . . service before you . . ."

Her eyes lifted abruptly to meet his. "I don't want to go back to being a parlormaid unless I have to," she said quickly.

"No, I understand that." He paused. "There is one other way you could help us, Miss Aylward."

"Yes? How?"

"Two missionaries have just returned from China. An old married couple who need someone to look after them. They have borrowed a house in Bristol. Would you be prepared to consider the job?"

She remembered how that offer had chilled her. Such a sad humiliation! Housekeeper to two retired missionaries too old to care for themselves! If that was the closest she was ever going to get to China, then perhaps it would be better if she did go back to her job as a parlormaid.

Gladys Aylward was an unmarried spinster of twenty-six, and the society into which she had been born expected her to work toward some small measure of security. It was usual, in those days between the two World Wars, if a young woman craved God, for her to sublimate that urge through attendance at church. But she also knew with certitude that the God to whom she owed allegiance wanted more from her than this milk-and-water reaction. She had gone straight from school into service and had moved from one parlormaid job to another. In those grim days of the "slump," if you had a job you stuck to it. But she was determined to make something more than that out of her life.

How the desire to go to China first arose she hardly knew

herself. It could have originated that evening when, bored and with nothing else to do, she had seen outside a local church a banner proclaiming a religious revival. Inside, a dynamic young clergyman exhorted his small audience to serve God. Her friends, seeing which way her inclinations were turning, declared quite bluntly that she was "barmy." "Don't be silly, Glad," they protested. "Come along to the pictures or to a dance, or let's go phone those nice chaps we met in the park." Suddenly, however, Gladys wanted more from life than that. She had joined a local evangelical society, and gradually the urge to go to China had eased into her mind. Eventually she had been accepted as a probationer at the China Inland Mission Center; and then in only a few months she had failed.

She worked for the elderly couple in Bristol, and soon after that managed to get a new job as a "Rescue Sister" on the docks at Swansea in South Wales. A rescuer of fallen women, and at twenty-six she hardly knew how they "fell" or what she was supposed to be rescuing them from! Night after night she patrolled the dock area. That she was only five feet tall and weighed about 110 pounds, and that drunken sailors, under the blotchy yellow street lights, were just as likely as not to mistake her for a prostitute and address her accordingly, did not really worry her. The younger girls, who had come by train from dark valley villages for a gay night out in the big city of Swansea, were usually grateful when Gladys put her thin arm around them and guided them off to a bed at the Mission hostel. Next morning they whispered their white-lipped thanks as she gave them a few coppers and put them on the train, to go home to face Biblical wrath in small cottages back in the Welsh mountains.

The older prostitutes, time-hardened by the economic pressures of the "slump," were different. They came to regard the young welfare worker, so eager and so full of the Lord, with tolerant amusement. Occasionally they even gave in to her appeals; several times on Sunday evenings she was able, triumphantly, to lead a party of them to Snelling's Gospel Mission.

Although these experiences had strengthened Gladys's spirit, they had added nothing to her bank balance. It became more and more obvious that if she was ever going to get to China—and she was determined to get there in some capacity or other, no matter what anyone might think—she would have to pay her own fare.

The only way she knew of earning money was to go back into service again. Reluctantly, she said good-by to her friends and returned to London.

An employment agency found her a post in the London home of Sir Francis Younghusband, the eminent soldier, author and explorer. Even now she remembered vividly her entry into the household. Dispirited after the long journey from the suburb of Edmonton, she knocked at the front door, and the butler showed her to her bedroom. It was small, neat and comfortable, but still a servant's bedroom. It was not China. She sat on the bed and looked at the small suitcase she had lugged upstairs. She took out the black, well-thumbed Bible and put it on the dressing table. She turned out her purse, which contained all the money she possessed. There were two pennies and one ha'penny. She placed the coins on top of the Bible. She felt like weeping. She was back where she had started . . . in service . . . and China seemed so far away. And, suddenly conscious of her deep need, she cried out: "Oh God, here's my Bible! Here's my money! Here's me! Use me, God!"

The door opened. A puzzled fellow housemaid who had been approaching and had heard the appeal, poked her head in. "Missus wants to see you in the drawing room," she said. "Always wants to see all the new staff as soon as they arrive."

"Thank you," said Gladys. She walked slowly downstairs.

Her mistress regarded the small, dejected figure curiously. "Miss Aylward . . . isn't it? I hope you'll be happy with me. Now, tell me, how much was your fare from home?"

"Two and ninepence," said Gladys. She did not understand the point of the question. Her mistress reached for her purse. "I always pay the fares of my maids when I engage them," she said. "Here's three shillings. The housekeeper will explain your duties later. . . ."

Renewed energy lifted Glady's heels as she hurried back upstairs. Exultantly, she spread out the three coins on her Bible. The bright silver shone against the black leather cover. Three shillings and twopence ha'penny! All to be hoarded against her fare to China. In spirit she was halfway there.

It was ironical, perhaps, that as Gladys Aylward dusted the books in the library of his stately Belgravia residence, Sir Francis Younghusband, the man who first crossed the heart of Central Asia by traversing the Mustagh Range, the great mountain barrier between Kashmir and China, was not even conscious of her presence. Yet she was to cross geographical and human terrain as formidable as any he ever faced.

She remembered, now, her first encounter with the ticket people. The elderly booking clerk at Mullers', the travel agency in the Haymarket, was quite certain she was mad. It seemed that in all his years of advising upon the pleasures of foreign travel, he had never heard such an outrageous demand. He had just finished patiently explaining that the cheapest boat fare to any portion of China was ninety pounds. He had pointed out, in passing, that *although* the cheapest and quickest route was overland through Europe, Russia and Siberia to Tientsin, via the Trans-Siberian Railroad—the fare for this journey being only forty-seven pounds, ten shillings—it was quite impossible to travel by that route. Yet this young woman facing him across the counter had chosen deliberately to misunderstand his words. She thrust three pound notes across at him, said she'd have a ticket on the railroad, and would he please accept this on account? He had tapped his slender fingers on the counter and adjusted his pince-nez to regard her more closely. A journey around the globe, a safari in Africa, a discreet week end in Le Touquet, they could all be managed. But this!

"As I was going to say, madam," he had said severely, "the journey by Trans-Siberian Railroad is quite impossible because a conflict between Russia and China is raging at the eastern end."

"I couldn't really care about a silly old war," she had said. "It's the cheapest way, isn't it? That's what I want. Now if you'll book me a passage, you can have this three pounds on account and I'll pay you as much as I can every week."

"We do not," the clerk had replied, choosing his words with the pedantic care of the extremely irritated, "like to deliver our customers . . . dead!"

His acidulousness had no effect whatsoever. She had stared up at him, quite logically feminine about it all. "Oh, they won't hurt me," she said. "I'm a woman. They won't bother about me."

It was three o'clock in the afternoon. Mullers' was almost empty. The clerk had time, therefore, to point out how important a communication link the Chinese Eastern Railroad was to the forces of both Russia and China. He explained that the Chinese, spurred on by the Young Marshal, Chang

22

Hsueh-liang, were trying to force the Russians to abandon their claims to the vital rail line which crossed Manchuria and connected with the Trans-Siberian Railroad. An undeclared war was in progress. Nothing could guarantee the safety of one young woman, even armed with that magical document, a British passport.

At the end of his speech, her dark brown eyes still regarded him steadily. The small hand in the worn glove still pushed the three pound notes in his direction. "It'll be all over by the time I get the rest of the money, I'm sure," she said. "If you'll order me a ticket I'll bring in my money every week until I've paid the balance. Is that all right?" The elderly clerk looked at her carefully. Then he sighed, picked up the three pounds and, defeated, reached for his receipt book. "Very well, madam," he said. "I don't know what the management would think about this, but I expect it will be all right."

Exactly what she thought she would be able to do when she arrived in China without a penny in her pocket, and not understanding a word of the language, she hardly knew herself. She was determined, nevertheless, that even if she could not pass through the scholastic eye of the China Inland Missionary needle, she could at least equip herself as an evangelist and know the Bible intimately. "I must learn to preach," she said to herself. "I must learn to talk to the people."

With the essential simplicity which characterized her, in every moment of spare time she went to Hyde Park, or to any street corner, where she mounted, literally, a soap box, and preached mainly to an iconoclastic and often a jeering audience. Tired Londoners moving tubeward in the evenings were startled to find themselves exhorted by a small girl in a black dress to turn, not homeward, but to God.

Against the clamor of London's traffic, her thin treble argued and pleaded, and although little more notice was taken of her than of the small blackbirds which festooned Nelson's Column, she was not disheartened.

She read, too, as much as she could, especially the stories of missionaries and books on China. From the local library, from the Younghusbands and from friends, she borrowed histories, volumes of sermons and other religious works. Thus she managed to plough through many of the books she had not had time to study at the China Inland Mission Center.

Then she had her first piece of luck. From a friend she heard of Mrs. Lawson. "A dear old soul, my dear. Seventy-three years old this year, and still working away as a missionary in China. She came back to England last year to retire, but she just couldn't stand it. So she returned to China—said she'd sooner end her days out there. She wrote only a few days ago saying she wished she could find some younger woman who could carry on with her work."

Gladys Aylward remembered how her mouth dropped open in astonishment, how all she could do was whisper weakly, "That's me! That's me!"

She wrote Mrs. Lawson at once. Could she help her? Could she join her? Could she come to China?

Now it became imperative that she save the money for the train ticket. In the Belgrave Square household she was willing to do anything. No chore was too long or arduous. She besieged employment agencies offering her services to work on her day off, to work week ends, to serve at banquets, to carry trays at society parties, to work all day and all night if necessary. By now the clerk at Mullers' was an old friend, accustomed to the enthusiastic young woman who appeared at his desk every Friday, bearing sums which would be counted out in pennies and shillings and entered against that magical total—forty-seven pounds, ten.

Then came that wonderful morning when the letter bearing the exotic Chinese stamps dropped with a plop on the hall floor. It told her that if she could manage to get to Tientsin by herself, a messenger would meet her there and guide her to wherever Mrs. Lawson was working.

She knew then that she had to get a passport at once. She had to finish paying for her ticket. "I'm going to China!" she said to all her friends. "I'm going to China!"

She would never forget the moment when that letter arrived, and the days of preparation that followed. . . .

And now, here she was . . . but just where was she? And what had happened? There had been the children, and the danger, with the river so wide, and the bullets so close. And now there were these white walls, and strange nurses, and tiredness and confusion, and a strange sort of peace. . . . Even if she died, right here in this room, she would die knowing that she had reached China—that her dream hadn't been just a dream after all.

CHAPTER TWO

GLADYS AYLWARD stood on the platform at Liverpool Street Station on Saturday, October 18th, 1930. She possessed in currency exactly ninepence in coin and two one-pound Cook's travelers' checks. The checks were sewed carefully into an old corset given to her by her mother, in the belief that even foreigners would not dare pry too closely into such an intimate and intimidating feminine accessory. The corset, in fact, was a treasure house. It contained, besides the travelers' checks, Gladys's Bible, her fountain pen, her tickets and her passport.

She kissed her mother and father and sister good-by, and settled herself into the corner seat of her third class compartment. The whistle blew, the train hissed and puffed; she waved through the window until her family were out of sight, then sat back and spread out on the seat beside her the old fur coat which a friend had given her and which her mother had cut up and made into a rug. Her two suitcases were on the rack. One held her clothes, the other an odd assortment of cans of corned beef, fish, and baked beans; crackers, soda biscuits and rye crisp; beef tea, powdered coffee, tea and hard-boiled eggs. She also had a saucepan, a kettle and an alcohol stove. The kettle and the saucepan were tied to the handle of the suitcase.

She took a boat at Hull, and disembarked at The Hague, tipped the porter who carried her bags the ninepence in coppers, and secured a corner seat on a continental train.

From Holland the train rattled across Germany, Poland and into the great steppes of Russia. She sat "facing the engine," cocooned in her fur rug, and watched the continent slide past. In Russia she was shocked by what she saw: the crowds of apathetic people waiting on the bare, cheerless stations; women working in gangs; poverty and peasantry on a scale she had not known existed.

The main station at Moscow was full of soldiers. They carried their bread ration under their arms, broke off a piece to munch when they felt hungry. To the young English girl cooking herself an egg, and having "elevenses" of beef tea, the rough-looking, bundled, bearded men who spat on the ground and blew their noses on their fingers were alien and a little horrible. She wrote, in letters which reached her mother, that she could not believe that Russia was happy; she suspected the people were downtrodden and wretched. The sight of small children working on the roads both saddened and sickened her. Once or twice a day she walked through the train corridor for exercise, and occasionally, when the engine stopped to take on wood, all the passengers disembarked to stretch their legs and replenish their water supply.

Ten days after she had left England, the train crossed into Siberia, and she was at once impressed by the grandeur of the scenery: the towering mountains, the great belts of dark pines, the endlessly stretching snow, the bright sunshine, and the immense loneliness. At one stop a man who could speak a little English came into her compartment, and, through him, the other passengers now began to ask questions of her. A kindly man, he conveyed to Gladys that the conductor who had examined her tickets wished to tell her that no trains were running to Harbin, and that she would probably be held up at the Siberian-Manchurian border. If this were true—and she concentrated on trying hard not to believe it—then her chances were remote of proceeding onward through Harbin to Dairen, and so by steamer to Tientsin.

To increase her fears, at each station stop more and more soldiers crowded onto the train. Two officers shared her compartment now, and although they could talk to her only in sign language, they were quite pleasant. At Chita all the other civilians left, and the conductor tried to persuade her to leave the train. But Gladys believed that every mile forward was a mile toward China, and refused to move.

Now the train filled up with troops and rumbled onward. A few hours later, in the darkness, it halted again at a tiny station and the soldiers got out, lined up on the platform and marched off up the track into the darkness. The train lights went out, and Gladys walked up the corridor and realized that she was the only person left aboard. Then came a noise, which, although she had never heard it before, she recognized immediately: the sound of gunfire. She poked her head out of the window and saw the distant flashes light the sky. Then she scrambled her belongings together, realizing, a little shamefacedly, that the elderly clerk at Mullers' had been right after all. There *was* a war on. And now she remembered the way he had said reprovingly, "But I did tell you, madam, that we do *not* like to deliver our customers dead."

Laden down by bags and rug, she wandered down the platform and, in a small hut near the track, found four men clustered around a stove: the engineer, the fireman, the station master, and the conductor who had tried to persuade her to get off the train at Chita. They made her a cup of strong coffee and with a running commentary translated by gymnastic gesticulations, repeated the fact that she had, indeed, reached the end of the line. Beyond was the battlefield.

28

This brief undeclared war between China and Russia over possession of the Chinese Eastern Railroad received little publicity in the western press. It lasted a few months, resulted in many casualties, and the Chinese eventually withdrew their forces. The train, the railroad men said, would remain at this stop for days, perhaps weeks, until such time as it was needed; then it would take wounded back to hospitals behind the line. They pointed down the track the way they had come. "Go back," they said.

The track wound drearily through snow-covered pines. It burrowed through dark tunnels; it was hemmed in by high mountains; the snow between the ties was thick and soft; icicles hung from the pine cones. But to walk back to Chita, they said, was her only hope.

And so she set off. She was not many miles from the Manchurian border. The Siberian wind blew the powdered snow around her heels, and she carried a suitcase in each hand, one still decorated ludicrously with kettle and saucepan. Around her shoulders she wore the fur rug. And so she trudged off into the night, a slight, lonely figure, dwarfed by the tall, somber trees, the towering mountains, and the black sky, diamond bright with stars. There were wolves near by, but this she did not know. Occasionally in the forest a handful of snow would slither to the ground with a sudden noise, or a branch would crack under the weight of snow, and she would pause and peer uncertainly in that direction. But nothing moved. There was no light, no warmth, nothing but endless loneliness.

Four hours later, when the cold and exhaustion became too much for her, she sat down on the icy rail, lit her alcohol stove and boiled some water for her powdered coffee. She ate two soda biscuits and felt miserable. She decided she must sleep at least for an hour or two. Arranging her suitcases into a windbreak, she wrapped herself up firmly in her old fur rug, and lay down. Drowsily, she listened to a chorus of far-off howling, and thought, "Now, I wonder who let all those big dogs out at this time of night?" Not until a couple of years later, in China, did she realize that she had heard a pack of hunting wolves.

A pale dawn was lighting the mountains when she awoke, stiff but refreshed. She made herself more coffee, ate another biscuit, gathered up her baggage and set off again along the interminable railroad track. Late that night, staggering along, almost unconscious with cold and weariness, she saw the lights of Chita gleaming far down the track. It gave her new strength. She struggled on, lifted herself wearily to the platform, dropped her suitcases into a heap and draped herself on top of them. There seemed to be nothing else to do, and she saw that several groups of Russians were doing the same thing.

During the night no one came near her, and Gladys dozed intermittently under her fur rug. Next morning a succession of station officials came to look at her, nod their heads and depart.

Nothing they said made sense to her, and so she continued to camp out on the platform in the bitter cold. Apparently no one cared. She dozed occasionally but now she was getting colder and stiffer. It seemed absurd to freeze to death on a Russian railroad platform. She decided to do something about it. Perhaps the only way to get anything done was to start a riot.

She eyed an official in a red cap coming along the platform toward her and wondered whether to kick him on the shin or knock off his imposing hat. Then she realized that violence was unnecessary, for the official was accompanied by three soldiers, and his objective was obviously herself. By gestures, he conveyed to her that she was under arrest, and must come with him.

Gathering up her baggage, she followed him along the platform and into a side room, which was so filthy and stank so abominably that she was almost sick. The door was locked and she was left there so long that she realized the Siberian cold of the platform was preferable. Finally the door was opened and she was led into another room. An interrogator managed to make her understand that he spoke English. He talked a long time but she could understand almost nothing of what he was trying to say. Eventually he left her, and she got out her fur rug. This room didn't smell so much—and under the bored eye of the soldier left to guard her she went fast asleep.

Next day the interrogation continued. They examined her shiny new passport and discussed interminably the entry that read: "Profession—Missionary." This, they seemed to be suggesting, had something to do with "machinery." They also hinted that she might like to stay in Russia; they had need of people like her.

During these years many young communists from all over the world were flocking to Soviet Russia, anxious to play their part in building a proletarian Utopia. That Gladys Aylward was mistaken for one of them is not surprising, but the mistake upset her. Hopefully, she thumbed through her Bible, which had colored pictures, and showed them Biblical scenes. This seemed to do some good, for after more discussion they handed her a paper, with official stamps on it, which seemed to be a new visa, also what looked like tickets for another journey.

That afternoon they escorted her to a train and managed to convey to her that she must change at a place called Nikol'sk-Ussuriyskiy. There she must catch a train for Sui-

31

fenho in Manchuria, which the Russians called Pogranichnaya, and so continue on to Harbin.

Eventually she disembarked at Nikol'sk-Ussuriyskiy. The
train to Pogranichnaya? No one spoke English. No one
understood. Finally, surrounded by her baggage, she settled
down to spend another night on the station platform. It was
so bitterly cold she thought she would freeze to death. Next
morning she brewed coffee on her alcohol stove, ate two of
the soda biscuits, parked her belongings at the station baggage room, and went off in search of some sort of government office, hoping she would find someone who spoke
English.

She found the government offices, but unfortunately, nobody spoke English. By now she was used to exhibiting her
Bible and drawing pictures. This time, however, in a moment of inspiration, she pulled out a picture of her brother,
Laurie, which showed him in the full dress of a drummer
in the British Army. By Russian standards in military uniforms, he looked like a major general. Whether or not they
thought she had high Army connections, she never learned,
but the picture produced instant and electrifying results. She
was whisked off, first to the station to collect her baggage,
then to a hotel where she spent the night. Next day she was
escorted to a train, her tickets were altered and she was re-
routed to Vladivostok. As she jolted through the interminable Siberian landscape, she offered up a little prayer of gratitude to brother Laurie.

On the platform at Vladivostok the collector examined
her ticket and let her out through the barrier. On the station
wall she saw a poster reading "Intourist Hotel" in Roman
lettering. Relieved, she decided to go there. By trying various phonetical intonations on passers-by, she eventually
reached its doors, and the hotel clerk signed her in. A thick-

set man with a pale Mongolian face, a creased suit and no collar, examined her passport and pocketed it. As far as Gladys could understand, he had something to do with the police. The words "O.G.P.U." meant nothing to her.

From then onward the police agent attached himself to her with a faithfulness that she found burdensome. He insisted on showing her the sights of Vladivostok, and what she saw horrified her: the filthy, unpaved roads full of water-filled potholes; lines of people outside food depots; the women in kimonos, eyes dark with hunger and weariness, babies on their backs; the shabby, unpainted buildings; the clattering streetcars jammed with unwashed, ragged passengers. That afternoon she stood with the man at a corner and watched one of these streetcars draw to a standstill. A thin, half-starved-looking woman ran to get on. The reason for the altercation that followed she never understood, but she saw the packed crowd of men on the car threatening the new passenger; then she saw them, just as the car was moving off, pick up the woman bodily and throw her into the roadway.

The woman fell with a thud and rolled over in the mud. The men screamed and jeered at her. Slowly the woman got up. She was weeping in such silent and bitter distress that Gladys's heart moved out to her. She took a step in her direction, but the man's hand on her arm restrained her. Her head bowed low, the woman trudged up the windy street after the streetcar. The impression of her body still remained in the mud.

Gladys was never afterward able to forget that episode. For her the cold wind which sifted through the streets, carrying on its breath the desolation of Siberia, was symbolic of Russia. Intuitively she understood the bewilderment and the hopelessness of its people. She could not express her feelings in a coherent, critical appraisal; she knew only how desperately she wanted to leave this country.

The next morning, the pale-faced agent was waiting outside her bedroom door. His unctuous attitude had somehow changed. As they went downstairs, she said, "Shall I be able to get my connection to Harbin soon?"

His dark eyes turned toward her.

"How can you get to China, anyway? You have no money to buy tickets."

Gladys was angry.

"I paid my fare from London to Tientsin," she said indignantly. "If your railroad people were honest, they'd see that I got there."

"But what is the point of going farther? You can work here just as well as in China. We need people like you who can handle machines and . . ."

"Machines! I've never worked a machine in my life."

"You should stay here," he said. "China is a long way off. We will see that you are taken care of."

Gladys saw very little as she walked through the streets of Vladivostok that morning. She was more worried now than she had been since the journey started. It seemed plain that this man had received instructions from someone to delay her.

As she entered the hotel foyer on her return, she was conscious that someone was walking close behind her. The O.G.P.U. man had gone back to his post at the desk. She glanced over her shoulder. It was a girl—dark, plainly dressed, but attractive. The girl drew level with her. Without turning her head she whispered in good if strongly accented English, "I must speak to you now. It is important. Follow me."

In mesmerized fashion, Gladys let the girl precede her,

and then followed into the corridor. The girl took her arm and steered her into a dark corner. "I waited until I was sure the O.G.P.U. man had left you," she said.

"But I don't understand. Who are you?"

"It doesn't matter. What matters is that you are in danger!"

"But I'm a British subject. I've got a passport."

"Where is it?"

"Here, in my bag."

"Take it out . . . open it."

Gladys fumbled in her bag, and suddenly remembered. The man at the desk: he had put it in his pocket and not returned it.

The girl's eyes were fixed on her, reading her thoughts. "They still have it? Then you must get it back! Here they need skilled factory workers desperately. If they decide to, they can send you off somewhere in the middle of Russia and you'll never be heard of again. Examine your passport carefully when they return it."

"Of course. But what am I to do?"

"I can help you."

"Help me? How can you help me?"

"Listen. Tonight after midnight be dressed and have your baggage ready. A knock will come on your door. Open it and follow the man outside. Do not speak to him. Simply follow him. You understand? But first ask them for your passport back."

Gladys nodded weakly, then stood in the dim corridor for a few moments after the girl had gone, trying to form a plan of action. She *had* to get the passport back. That was essential. She walked back to the desk in the foyer. The O.G.P.U. man was sitting on a tilted chair smoking a cigarette. He looked contemptuously up at her.

35

"My passport?" said Gladys. "I would like my passport back."

He rocked his chair back to floor level, took the cigarette out of his mouth, and blew out smoke. "It is still being examined. I will bring it to you—this evening."

"Thank you," said Gladys, and walked quickly away.

That night she sat in the cold bedroom after eating her supper. A knock came on the door. She walked across and opened it. It was the O.G.P.U. man, grinning, waving the passport tantalizingly in one hand. He put his foot in the door. Instinctively warned, with a quick movement she reached up, snatched the passport from his hand, and flicked it over her head into the bedroom. The bitter, sardonic grin on his face frightened her. He forced the door wide open and stepped inside.

"Don't you dare come in here!" she said. "Get out! Get out at once!"

"I am coming in and you can't stop me." His slitted eyes flicked across to the bed and back to her.

She was so petrified with astonishment that she allowed him to take three steps toward her. Then she leaped backward, exclaiming unsteadily: "God will protect me! God will protect me!"

The man stopped. He seemed puzzled. For a moment he stared at her, rooted so dramatically in front of him, then he started to grin. The grin turned into a laugh, finally into a roar of laughter. Astonished but implacable, Gladys glared at him. Abruptly his mood changed. He swore at her savagely, cursed her in Russian and English. He lifted his hand threateningly, thought better of it, and stepped backward out of the door, slamming it behind him. Gladys dived at the bolt and thrust it home. She leaned back against the door, pressing her palms against it, and she realized that she had to get out of the hotel that very night.

Hurriedly she picked up her passport. What had the girl said—something about examining it? She opened it, flipped through the pages. Her finger trembled with fright as she saw what they had done. The word "Missionary" had been altered to "Machinist." She closed it, crammed it into her bag, hauled her suitcases from under the bed and piled in her belongings. Then she sat on the bed waiting for midnight, praying that the girl had told the truth. Or was her story some part of an artful plan to trap her? Now she didn't care. She had to take a chance. She had to get away.

The knock was so gentle that she barely heard it. She hesitated before unlocking the door, then decided she must go through with it. A strange man in a drab mackintosh and wilted hat stood outside. It was so dark she could hardly see his face. He motioned to her to come out and held the door open while she bundled through with her suitcases. Then he went on ahead and she followed him along the corridor, down the stairs and past the reception desk. The clerk was nodding in his chair by the stove; there was no sign of the O.G.P.U. man. The revolving door grated a little as it spun around, and she had difficulty with her cases. Then they were out in the cold night air.

She walked quickly after the stranger, stumbling into potholes in the unlit streets. As they hurried through dark side streets, she had a feeling that they were approaching the sea. Against the night sky she could see the thin shapes of dockside cranes. Soon they were stumbling over railroad tracks embedded in cobblestones. From the shadow of a pile of packing cases stepped another figure. It was the girl, and with a sigh of thankfulness Gladys hurried to her. The man stepped back into the shadows.

"I am glad you have come," the girl said.

"What do I do now?" Gladys asked anxiously.

"You see that ship." The girl pointed to the black bulk of a freighter looming beyond the dark sheds and cranes.

"Yes."

"It is a Japanese ship. It sails for Japan at dawn. You must be on it."

"But Japan! I've got no money. . . ." Gladys's voice rose into a wail.

"You'll find the captain of the ship in that small wooden hut over there. You must go and see him. Plead with him, tell him you are in great trouble. You *must* leave on that ship. . . ."

"All right, I'll try."

The girl stood there in the darkness, and Gladys did not know how to thank her. "What about you? I haven't even thanked you for what you have done. Why have you helped me like this?"

"You needed help." The girl's voice was low and sad.

"But you?"

"I live here. I shall be all right."

"But how can I thank you? What can I give you? I have no money. . . ."

"It does not matter."

Gladys sensed the hesitation in the girl's voice.

"There is something?"

"You have perhaps . . . clothes?"

Every garment Gladys possessed she was wearing against the bitter cold. She had nothing except what she wore, but she had to show her gratitude somehow. She whipped off her gloves.

"Here, take these, please. And these stockings." She fumbled in her coat pocket and produced a pair she had thrust there in her hurry.

"They're old and darned, but please have them."

The girl took them. "Thank you," she said quietly. "Good luck!" Their hands touched for a moment in the darkness. Then she turned on her heel and walked away, her feet echoing on the cobblestones.

Gladys pushed open the door of the little hut. A naked electric bulb hung from the roof, and a bare wooden table was piled with papers. On the other side of it sat a young Japanese in merchant marine uniform. He looked up gravely as she came in.

"Please," she said, "are you the captain of that boat? I'm English and I must get on it. I *must* get on it."

He stared at her impassively. Then he said in excellent English, "How are you? Please speak slowly. What is it you wish?"

"I want to go to Japan on your ship."

"Indeed! Have you money to pay your fare?"

"No. Nothing!"

His black eyes were unblinking and quite incurious.

"No valuables of any sort?"

"No, nothing at all. But I must leave here. I must!" The captain nodded his head. His face had shown not the slightest sign of emotion.

"You say you are a British subject? You have a passport?"

Gladys fished her passport out of her bag and handed it to him. He leafed through it carefully. As she watched him, she had a feeling that he had done this many times.

"A British subject in trouble. We really cannot have that, can we? Yes, I will take you on my ship. There are some papers you must sign, that is all. If you will come with me, I will find you a cabin."

39

Six hours later, as dawn was coloring the bare red hill-sides along the coastline, the Japanese steamship slowly slid out toward the open ocean, with Vladivostok a smudge of smoke behind them. At the rail Gladys Aylward looked back at the city she was leaving. She felt as if she had spent a life-time crossing Russia and Siberia, and only through great good fortune had managed to escape. She wondered who the girl was who had helped her, the man who had knocked at her door. She knew she would never meet them, either of them, again, that they would always remain eternal enigmas in her past. But she wished them luck, for she felt that, already, she herself had received a fair allowance of that glittering, fateful currency.

CHAPTER THREE

THREE DAYS after leaving Vladivostok they steamed into the small port of Tsuruga on the west coast of Japan. Farther to the south was Kobe and from there, the captain explained, she would be able to catch a boat to China. He also informed her that she would have to wait on board while he got in touch with the British Consul or his representative.

Not long after they docked, therefore, a rather disconcerted but extremely pleasant young Englishman arrived to interview her. After a few questions, he conveyed both her and her baggage to a small restaurant near the dock area "where they could talk properly." He was obviously embarrassed by the encounter. He said, "It's all rather difficult. I wonder what we can do for you now?"

"I shall be quite all right when I reach Kobe," said Gladys firmly. After her adventures in the U.S.S.R., she was confident that if you repeated your desires often enough, and firmly and convincingly enough, something was bound to happen.

The young man's surprise showed in his face. "In that case I'll get you a ticket to Kobe and put you on a train straight away," he said quickly.

On the train, in the inevitable corner seat, she watched the countryside go by, contrasting the beauty and delicacy of the landscape with the savage disorderliness of the continent she had just left.

On the landward side, faraway, high, snow-covered peaks shaded down to green hills and fertile fields. On the other, green islands toppled into a blue, sun-bright sea. Tiny sailboats poised in silhouette against the glare of sea and sky. They passed shady villages of tile-roofed houses, and trees aflame with scarlet blossom. In the fields the rice was golden ripe, waiting for the sickle, and at every stop chattering groups of Japanese people in clean, bright shirts and kimonos bundled on and off the train.

Afterward Gladys Aylward never could reconcile, or equate in mind or memory, the attractive, happy people she had met in Japan with the outrageous warriors she was to know with such horrifying intimacy in later years.

On the platform at Kobe, she went to the Japanese Tourist Bureau, changed one of her pound travelers' checks and received a bewildering assortment of *yen*. She walked out into the dazzle of bright autumn sunshine. Before she could protest, she was seized on by a rickshaw boy, piled, with her luggage, into his flimsy two-wheeled vehicle, and borne at top speed through the traffic-filled streets of Kobe.

She gazed eagerly at the crowds, the open bazaars, the narrow alleyways hung with bright banners inscribed with gold and scarlet characters. Suddenly she remembered that back in London she had heard about a Japanese Christian organization, "The Japanese Evangelistic Band." She was still trying to recall more about this when she saw, hanging outside one hall, a notice board bearing a cross and the words, "Kobe Mission Hall."

Possibly her rickshaw boy, with a knowledge of humanity born of experience, had deliberately taken her in this direction, for at her shrill exclamation he trotted obediently over to the door. Inside, a pleasant Japanese directed her rickshaw boy to the house of the Dyers, the English missionaries in charge, who were delighted to meet their unexpected caller. They listened to the story of her adventures, and Mr. Dyer frowned as he heard of the circuitous way in which she had reached Japan.

"But if you paid for tickets to Tientsin, the travel people should get you there, no matter how you were diverted," he said. "Give me all the tickets you have left and I'll see the agency people here tomorrow."

They gave her a bath in a large wooden tub, Japanese style, and then put her to bed in a pretty room lit by a Japanese lantern of red and blue. It was the first good night's sleep she had had since leaving England.

Next morning, after a session with Cook's tourist agency, Mr. Dyer reappeared bearing an envelope containing a steamship ticket from Kobe to Tientsin which they had agreed to exchange for Gladys's unused vouchers.

Three days later, from the deck of a neat little Japanese ship, she stared across the muddy yellow sea at a dark purple smudge on the horizon. Behind it the sun was setting with gaudy flamboyance, and she stared at it until all the color had left the sky. For this was China.

At Tientsin she found a large mission with a European staff. Yes, they had heard of Mrs. Lawson. As far as they knew, she was in Shansi province, in northwest China, at a mission station in an old walled town called Tsechow. It was north of the Yellow River, in very wild and mountainous territory. It would take many weeks to get there. They would ask around and see if they could find a guide who could take her part way into the interior. Meanwhile, they would be glad to put her up.

Seven days later, as the train pulled out of Tientsin station, away from the sprawl of Westernized suburbs, Gladys felt the pulse of the wheels echo her own excitement. Mr. Lu, a sober young man in a dark Chinese robe, with a fedora on his head, was to accompany her for part of the journey. He had business in Shansi; he was also a Christian. She had changed her last travelers' check in order to buy a Chinese pass which permitted her to go inland. It had cost twelve shillings, leaving her with very little money indeed. This did not really worry her, as the train jogged slowly across the flat, featureless landscape. It was a bright day in late autumn. The fields were now denuded of the harvest and the light shone on the short golden stubble. Soon, along the western horizon, an immense semicircle of purple mountains rose against the sky. The countryside lost its flat dullness. The train chugged across fertile agricultural country, past farms and mud-walled villages backed by clumps of trees. There were cemeteries enclosed by gray stone walls and entered through magnificent ornamental gates, where lay the generations of well-loved worshipful ancestors. Along open roads sunk in the soft, fruitful earth the blue-garmented, pigtailed peasants drove their heavy, two-wheeled carts drawn by shaggy Mongolian ponies.

Mounted on these beasts, Mr. Lu told Gladys, the horde of Jenghiz Khan's Tatars had driven south to extend their empire. It was against successive waves of similar invaders that the fifteen-hundred-mile long Great Wall of China had been built. Men might scale the wall; horses never. Mounted, the Tatars raided as swiftly and devastatingly as locusts. Deprived of horses, they were small men with bandy legs, and the Chinese were a match for them.

Gladys Aylward was enchanted by the countryside. At the stops as they neared Peking, flower sellers thrust bunches of pink or white lotus blossoms through the windows. The feeling of immemorial continuity overwhelmed her. Yes, it was alien: that still distant barrier of savage mountains, the occasional swaying, tan-colored caravans of Gobi camels, and eventually the soaring, square-bastioned walls of Peking, with their great bell towers, a city of temples and pagodas, statues and calm pools reflecting the leaves of the lotus flower. But every new scene excited her.

They spent that night at a Chinese inn in Peking, and went on again by train the next morning. The railroad line ended three days later at Yutsa. From there on they made progress by means of ramshackle old buses. Each night they stopped at an inn. Privacy had disappeared; everyone slept on the *k'ang,* the communal brick bed under which flowed hot air from the stove. No one undressed; everyone endeavored with philosophical calm to preserve a few inches of flesh from the foraging and hungry fleas and lice.

The province of Shansi is cut off in the south and west by the Yellow River, the Hwang Ho. This mighty river rises in the distant province of Tsinghai and forces its way across three thousand miles of China's soil before it spews into the ocean in Shantung province with such power that ships' crews sixty miles out notice the turgid yellow coloration. To the north and east, Shansi is protected by high masses of barren mountains. The province is the home of Chinese agriculture, the cradle of Chinese civilization. Its Fen River valley has been cultivated continuously for over four thousand years. Millet, wheat and barley, crops requiring little moisture, have always grown there in a wild state. In northwest China the people eat grain rather than rice to this day, as Gladys discovered at the inns, where boiled dough strings formed the basis of all meals.

A month after leaving Tientsin, Gladys arrived at Tsechow, the city where the Tientsin missionaries had told her she would find Mrs. Lawson. Two old ladies, one of whom was a Mrs. Smith, ran the mission there. They were both about seventy years old. Mrs. Smith's husband had been a missionary for many years; after his death she had decided to stay on, and had been joined by her friend, a nurse. They told Gladys that Mrs. Lawson had stayed with them for several weeks. Then she had moved into the wild, mountainous area to the west, country into which Christianity had never penetrated. It was forbidding terrain; the villages were isolated, the small towns walled and fortified. They had heard that Mrs. Lawson was living for the time being at Yangcheng, a walled town which lay two days' journey away, along the ancient mule track from Honan to Hopeh.

"How do I get there?" asked Gladys wearily. The long days of traveling had worn her out.

Mrs. Smith was the kind of old lady one finds in tea shops in Bath and Harrogate, but rarely several hundred miles from anywhere in the middle of China. Her gentle good looks, however, concealed an extreme competence. A niece of Archbishop Lang, she was a very talented woman with a great gift for the Chinese language and dialects. She peered at Gladys through her spectacles.

"My dear, the only way is by mule through the mountains," she said. "The road ends here. Only tracks lead onward. It's very rough going and there are immense stretches of lonely country. It's a day's journey to Chowtsun, the first village, and then another day on to Yangcheng."

"I'll start tomorrow if I can," said Gladys.

Mrs. Smith looked at her thoughtfully. "I wouldn't wear those European clothes either, if I were you, my dear," she suggested kindly. Gladys looked down at her soiled red frock and coat. "But it's all I've got."

"We'll find you others," said Mrs. Smith. "You see, there

46

are bandits in the mountains. They would know you are a foreigner and might think you were rich. We can fit you out with the blue jacket and trousers that everybody wears. Where you are going, they've never seen a European woman before. They're very simple, primitive people; they think all foreigners are devils! It's better not to draw too much attention to yourself."

At first light next morning, seated uncomfortably inside a mule litter, a canopied platform secured on the animal's back, and accompanied by a muleteer, Gladys started her journey. For nine miles they traveled over the plain, and then the narrow, flinty path turned up into the mountains. Before dark they had reached Chowtsun, where they were breaking their trip.

No one traveled at night in this region. The paths were too steep and precipitous, and travelers feared both bandits and wolves in the high country. Chowtsun, secure within its walls, was full of inns and shouting children and teams of mules and muleteers.

At dawn they were off again, winding along a narrow path hacked from the mountainside. The clip-clop of the mules' hoofs on the flinty track echoed in the clear air. High overhead a pair of eagles soared lazily in the first sunlight. Seven hours later, rounding a bend in the trail, the muleteer pulled his animals to a halt and pointed with a grimy forefinger. "Yangcheng," he said.

The city stood far off on its mountain peak like a castle in a fairy tale. Its high walls grew from the natural rock, and delicate pagodas and temples, still only silhouettes, but made more mysterious by distance, rose high above the walls. Against the satin sky of late afternoon it gave her an impression of unattainable beauty. Weary as she was, Gladys felt her spirit lifted up at the sight. As they drew nearer she saw

47

that, among the otherwise barren mountains, there were two quite close to the city that were covered with trees and dense foliage. The trail passed over one, tunneling through green shade until it came out into the hard sunlight again and climbed steeply to the East Gate. On all sides, from that altitude, glorious panoramas of mountain and valley rolled away into the distance. Gladys was enthralled by the natural grandeur. She had never suspected that such a place existed.

Yangcheng has sat there on its mountain saddle, a tiny island of Confucian civilization astride the ancient track between Honan and Hopeh, longer than man can remember, or history has recorded. The mule track passes in through the East Gate and out through the West. On three sides the country falls away steeply, but there are inns and cave dwellings on the slopes. On the south side it falls sheerly, thousands of feet to the wild valley below. At nightfall all gates are locked, and mule trains arriving after that hour are refused admittance to the city. They cannot pass forward, and must find shelter for the night in one of the inns in the shadow of the walls or on the slopes.

At the East Gate, Gladys's muleteer halted and questioned one of the old men sitting there in the sun. He pointed to the narrow roadway that turned down left outside the city wall. The muleteer urged the beasts toward it. A hundred yards down the track, lined on both sides by the blank courtyard walls of private houses and inns, he stopped and indicated a building. The tired mules nosed in toward the narrow entrance to the courtyard, their hoofs clattering on the stones.

Out of the door to meet them came a small lady with white hair and the bluest eyes Gladys had ever seen. She was dressed in a plain blue robe and trousers. She looked up at Gladys and asked abruptly, "Who are you?"

"I'm Gladys Aylward. You're Mrs. Lawson?"

"Yes, I am. Well, come on in."

The brusque reception did not startle Gladys; she was accustomed to the extraordinary by now. The muleteer helped her off the litter and she followed Mrs. Lawson into the house.

Like most Chinese dwellings, it was square, enclosed by four high walls. From a square recess in the front wall, a small door led inward to a large courtyard. The rooms of the two-storied dwelling opened onto balconies which overlooked the courtyard. The house was almost a wreck. Practically every door was off its hinges; there were piles of rubble on the flagstones, gaping holes in the tiled roof, dirt everywhere.

"I've only just managed to rent it," said Mrs. Lawson. "Got it cheap because it's haunted. It's a bit rough, but it'll be all right when it's cleaned up."

Gladys followed her into what appeared to be the only habitable place. In the room stood a table and a couple of chairs. There was no other furniture except a few odd packing cases and soap boxes.

"Are you hungry?" asked Mrs. Lawson.

"Famished," said Gladys weakly.

Mrs. Lawson called out in Chinese, and an old man came in. He was introduced as "Yang, the cook."

Yang smiled at her; he was an old Chinese with a toothless smile. Gladys immediately warmed to him. A few moments later he brought a large bowl of the inevitable boiled dough strings into which had been mixed some chopped vegetables. She ate ravenously. After the meal she went out to get her baggage, and to look at the view. As she turned through the courtyard doorway, a group of small Chinese children saw her and fled, howling. Some older children appeared over a wall, surrounded her and began to jeer in singsong voices. Two women farther down the street picked up pieces of dried mud and flung them in her direction. In consternation Gladys walked quickly back to Mrs. Lawson and told her what had occurred.

"It happens to me every time I go out," said Mrs. Lawson calmly. "I usually come back covered from head to foot with the filth and mud they've thrown at me. So far, it hasn't been stones, thank goodness. They hate us here. They call us *lao-yang-kwei*, foreign devils. It's something you'll have to get used to."

CHAPTER FOUR

JEANNIE LAWSON was five feet tall, seventy-four years old, and in appearance rather frail. It was a deceptive appearance. Her pure white hair, an odd phenomenon in China, convinced every peasant in Yangcheng that she was not only a foreign devil, but also an evil spirit. This hair terrified them wherever she went, a fact which did not trouble Jeannie Lawson in the slightest. She had arrived in China as a young girl of twenty-one, married another missionary, borne her children, seen her first-born die of the black fever, and watched the others grow up and go into the world. She had outlived her husband by many years.

She was Scottish. Her ancestors had fought for centuries against the invading English, and spiritually she was determined to brandish the word of God in the face of all unbelievers. Not for her the tame Christianity of the plains with its Bible classes, needlework and issues of aspirin; in these mountains there were heathens to be shown the light of God, and Jeannie's self-appointed task was to seek them out and show it to them. If Chinese urchins followed them in mocking groups every time they walked in the streets, and women slammed their doors and spat, and men hurled mud, it must all be endured in true Christian fashion; eventually she would find a way to come to grips with them. If there was ever a militant Christian abroad in the mountains of Shansi, it was Jeannie Lawson.

Gladys, in those first early weeks, found life harder to

51

bear. Possessing a personal fortune of exactly five shillings, many thousands of miles from her homeland, speaking no word of the language, spat upon and reviled every time she moved from the house, she often came home in tears to wash the mud off her clothes. She remembered with nostalgia the scores of neat little Japanese converts she had seen at the mission in Kobe, clean and smiling and virtuous, singing their psalms and hymns so prettily.

Yangcheng was not remotely like that. One day, quite early in her stay, the difference was made plain to her. She was walking through the city. Within the walls the townspeople had become more or less accustomed to the "foreign devils" by now, and while they still moved out of their path, it was too much trouble to keep throwing mud. As Gladys walked toward the market square she saw a crowd gathering. Then she saw the Chinese woman who lived in the house next door and smiled at her occasionally. The woman beckoned excitedly, and as Gladys, pleased by this sudden indication of friendship, came up, she grabbed her wrist and hurried with her through the crowd. "Jugglers," thought Gladys excitedly, "or perhaps a man with a performing bear." It was fairly common to see such strolling players performing in the market square.

The impetus of their rush took them right through the crowd to the front rank. Gladys was puzzled by what she saw. A man, shaven-headed, his pigtail looped around his forehead, stood there. He was bent forward, his shoulders hunched in a queer, almost pathetic, manner. A soldier, his back to Gladys, stood close to him. In bewilderment she stared, sensing the tragic, suddenly wide-eyed as she saw the bright flash of a curved execution sword, swung high in the air. Petrified, she glimpsed the blade poised aloft, burnished by the sun; shocked beyond comprehension, she watched it slash downward. Rigid, in utter horror, she saw the blade strike home, and the jetting spurt of scarlet blood arch upward and splash softly on the flagstones. A gusty moan of suppressed excitement came from the crowd as the head bounced and rolled. Gladys jerked her wrist free from the hand of the Chinese woman, who was completely obsessed by the scene, turned and forced her way frantically through the milling, jabbering onlookers. She raced back through the streets, deserted now, for everyone had hurried to see the execution. With tears streaming down her face, she doubled around through the East Gate and ran down to the house.

Jeannie Lawson was sitting at the table writing in her journal when Gladys burst in, almost incoherent with grief and shock.

"Whatever's the matter?" said Jeannie, surprised.

"I've just seen a dreadful thing, a most dreadful thing," sobbed Gladys. "They've killed a man in the market square with a sword."

With deliberation, Jeannie, veteran of over fifty years in China, placed her pencil down at the side of her notebook.

"Well?" she demanded, curtly. Gladys's face was streaked with tears. She blinked with astonishment.

"But they cut off his head with a sword!"

Jeannie's gaze was still steady. "It is the law for certain crimes. He was probably a bandit, or a thief or a murderer. He must have been tried before the Mandarin in the *yamen*. If they're found guilty, they chop off their heads straight away, more often than not."

"But it's horrible!"

"Did you expect things to be the same in China as in England?"

"No, but . . ."

53

"Listen to me, Gladys Aylward, you haven't come here to China to alter their laws. They'll throw the body down the mountainside where it will be eaten by wolves or carrion birds. There'll be no Christian burial, understand that," she added, sparing her nothing. "And they'll stand the head up on the city wall so that everyone can see it."

"It's so awful—so feudal!"

"Yes, it's feudal. Sometimes they won't have an execution for months. Then suddenly there's a batch, and the whole wall's lined with heads. You may as well get used to it. There are a lot of things in China you'll have to get used to. We'll try to change these things through the love and wisdom of Jesus Christ, by making them understand truth and justice, but we won't do it by running home blubbering our eyes out."

Gladys had no reply to that, but despite Jeannie's words she never forgot the horror of that scene. In the future, she would see worse sights, but the memory of that execution, even in the years which followed, demonstrated and dramatized for her the odd streak of cruelty which, she decided, must lie deep in even the most civilized Chinese.

It was a period of "settling in." Jeannie Lawson explained her financial position. She had a small private income; the rent for the house, because it was old and dilapidated, and according to local legend full of ghosts and evil spirits, worked out in British currency at two shillings and fourpence a year. Millet, wheat and vegetables cost only a few *cash*. The value of *cash*, the small copper coins with holes in the center for stringing them together, was two hundred to the Chinese dollar, which then stood at about one shilling and twopence. Financially, they were reasonably secure; but what was the use of security if they could not do the job for which they were both in China?

54

They arrived at the brilliant idea one day as they were walking back up the slope to the West Gate. They passed through the narrow main street and skirted the *yamen,* or town hall, where the Mandarin lived and all the official business of the city was carried out. Narrow alleyways led off in all directions from the main road, and inside the strong arms of the wall, the life of the city bubbled noisily.

The early mule trains were already coming through the gates to find lodging at the inns within the city walls. The whole purpose of Yangcheng's existence through the centuries had been as a fortified stopping place for mule caravans and travelers who passed along an important trading route. So great was the traffic that many inns had grown up outside the city walls, and every night Yangcheng was packed with muleteers and carriers.

As the mule trains passed by, Gladys voiced her thoughts. "If we could only talk to these men, they'd carry our message for hundreds of miles through the province."

Jeannie Lawson walked on without a word for several paces. Then suddenly she rounded on Gladys.

"You've put your finger right on it," she said. "We'll open an inn."

Gladys stared at her, thinking she had not heard correctly.

"Open an inn?" she repeated incredulously.

"Of course! Why didn't I think of it before? Our house was built as an inn in the first place, hundreds of years ago. We've plenty of rooms. There are three *k'angs* specially constructed to sleep large numbers, two downstairs, one in the large room upstairs. We'll have to get the roof mended. We could put up at least fifty men and their animals. We've got a cook. It's quite easy to feed them." Her voice was full of enthusiasm.

55

"But we didn't come here to be innkeepers," said Gladys dubiously.

"Don't you see what I'm after?" said Jeannie impatiently. "Once we've got them inside we can tell them stories of the Gospels. The Chinese love stories. All the inns offer roughly the same service, a bed and food; we can only charge the same price, two *cash* a night, but as an added inducement we shall tell them stories. It's a wonderful idea!" She began to walk forward again. "Now, the first thing we've got to do is get that roof repaired. Then we'll have to get food in. . . ."

Gladys was carried along on the flood tide of this enthusiasm. Yang, the cook, said he thought it a good idea; he was a mild old man with a mountaineer's wrinkled face and a sharp peasant intelligence, and if he said it was feasible, then it was.

The roof was mended; the large courtyard was cleaned out. New doors were fixed to the rooms. The balustrade around the second floor balcony was rebuilt. The windows were repaired; as the panes were only made of translucent paper, that wasn't too difficult. Large quantities of millet and corn and vegetables were soon stored.

"A name," said Jeannie. "We must have a signboard outside the house giving the name of the inn. They all do."

"I suppose we could call it the Red Lion or the White Hart," said Gladys, "though I think my mother would be a bit shocked if she thought I'd come all the way to China to work as a barmaid in the Red Lion."

Jeannie Lawson laughed. "I've got it," she said. "A wonderful name. . . . The Inn of Eight Happinesses. Isn't that good?"

"It sounds more Oriental than the Red Lion, I must admit," said Gladys.

A sign painter was commissioned to do the job, and eventually the narrow yellow signboard painted with Chinese characters in black and gold hung outside their house. The name followed the true tradition of classical Chinese nomenclature, which encourages the flowery and euphonious. No one in Yangcheng thought it odd.

Soon the inn was officially open. The smell of good food eddied out from Yang's kitchen, and they waited patiently for the first customers. Muleteers crowded into the inn opposite and those farther down the street. Muleteers and carriers plodded past, looking up at the inviting appeal of the Inn of Eight Happinesses, but no one came into the hostelry of the foreign devils. Obviously they were being boycotted. Jeannie held a council of war, and decided that more seductive, or forceful, measures would have to be taken.

"You," said Jeannie, leveling a finger at Gladys, "will be responsible for bringing the customers into the courtyard."

"But how?" protested Gladys. "If they don't want to come into *our* courtyard, how can I get them in?"

"It isn't a case of their *wanting* to come in," said Jeannie positively. "You've got to drag them in."

"Drag them in?" Gladys's voice was at least one octave above normal. Jeannie Lawson chattered questioningly in Chinese to Yang. He nodded his bald head in agreement. "*Ai-ai,*" he said.

Apparently, according to him, there was a psychology attached to bringing a customer to bed in a Yangcheng hostelry that was unique in the accommodation business. Some of the more staid muleteers made reservations at the same inn every time they passed through. You did not try to poach them; that was unethical. But there were many other casual visitors. When a muleteer came down the track looking to left and right at the inn signs, you took it that he was a casual. Legitimate prey! Then the innkeeper, who stood bland and benign at his courtyard door, went into action. As the lead mule passed he made a grab at the animal's head and tried to drag it in the direction of his own courtyard. The mules behind the lead mule were all tied to it with no choice but to follow. That, said Jeannie Lawson, was going to be Gladys's job.

"But what if they bite me!" Gladys protested.

"Now, don't be stupid," said Jeannie. "You're the youngest and most active. I'm too old. Yang will be busy with the food. You'll have to do it."

Instead of being bitten, Yang explained, Gladys would be aided and abetted by the sagacious mules. The poor beasts, after a hard day on the mountain trails, were only too anxious to be unloaded, and given food and water. Experience told them that once they got their heads inside a courtyard in the late afternoon or early evening, work was over. They were there to stay. No tidbit, promise or enticement would lure them out again until next morning. Therefore, any tugging of the lead rein in the direction of a courtyard doorway would be met on their part by complete approval. Jeannie Lawson did not think they would put up much resistance even when a "foreign devil" grabbed their reins.

The next evening, bolstered by this knowledge and equipped with a sales call which she was to cry out to the passing muleteers, Gladys stood gloomily at the doorway of the inn and waited for business. The inducement she offered, a sentence in which she had been carefully coached by Yang, announced: *"Muyo beatch—muyo goodso—how—how—how —lai—lai—lai."* ("We have no bugs, we have no fleas, good, good, good, come, come, come!")

Gladys tried it out on the first three mule trains which clopped past her. Neither animals nor muleteers took the slightest notice. It was plain that there was no magic in the words. Anxiously she realized that physical assault was also necessary.

With hands tucked into the wide sleeves of her coat, the hereditary stance adopted by all Chinese innkeepers, this young English girl stood in the shadow of the doorway. A mule train clip-clopped slowly down the street. The muleteer was obviously tired, lagging a yard or two behind his lead animal. The mule came level and Gladys ran forward. So enthusiastic was her leap that its momentum carried her past the mule's head into full view of the muleteer. In the half light he recognized her at once as a "foreign devil," and screamed in terror, but he had the lead rein firmly tied to his wrist and could not escape. Gladys, recovering her balance, jerked at the mule's head and found herself borne into the courtyard astride the nose of the weary beast, the muleteer being dragged in along with his team. Hoofs struck sharply on the flagstones, steam rose from the mules' flanks; they gathered in a tired group.

Gladys looked at them in awe. She had never been so close to the front end of a mule before, not even on the journey from Tsechow. She put out her hand and patted a velvet muzzle. Brown eyes looked at her in reproach. "Packs off," they intimated, "fodder, water?" Gladys had captured a mule train singlehanded, but only one man. The others had all fled.

At that moment, Jeannie and Yang came out of the kitchen.

"Well done," said Jeannie, hopping with delight. "Indeed, well done!"

That did it: the muleteer had regarded Gladys with awe; the sight of the white-haired spirit advancing on him was too much. He tore the lead rein from his wrist and, with a shriek, bolted from the courtyard.

59

'Now look what you've done!" wailed Gladys. "At least we had one man. Now you've frightened him away, too!"

Jeannie Lawson clapped her on the back. "Don't worry, they dare not leave these mules; they're much too valuable. They'll be back, you'll see."

Yang was dispatched up to the city gate to find the muleteers, reassure them and bring them to the inn.

Ten minutes later he returned, and one dubious Chinese crept fearfully into the courtyard after him. Yang had explained that the "foreign devil" ladies offered clean accommodation, good food and, as an extra attraction, stories which were to be told free of charge, all this at the cheap rate of two *cash* a night. Where else in the whole province of Shansi could such a bargain be found? What was there to fear? Was not he, Yang, an old and respected Chinese, living with the "foreign devils"? And he had not been bewitched! Let the muleteer spend but one night at this inn of the utmost comfort and find out for himself. Yang knew, as did the muleteer, that no human agency could lure the mules out of the courtyard until next morning, and that there was nothing else to do but make the best of it. The muleteer collected his helpers. They unfastened the packs, watered and fed the tired animals, and went into the large downstairs room where the heated *k'ang* ran the entire length of one wall. Yang brought in the steaming cauldron of food and slopped it into their basins. They ate hungrily and agreed that it was good food, but when Jeannie Lawson and Gladys entered there was a perceptible movement toward the farthest corner of the room.

Jeannie was unabashed. She had her audience. "Don't be afraid," she said cheerfully. "I want to tell you a story which you will enjoy. All the stories we tell at the Inn of Eight Happinesses are free." The men looked a little more interested and Jeannie perched herself on the stool she had brought in with her. "The story I am going to tell you tonight," she said, "concerns a man called Jesus Christ. He lived long ago in a faraway country called Palestine. . . ."

The inn was open. The storytelling had begun.

CHAPTER FIVE

THEIR SUCCESS as innkeepers was hard-earned. Evening after evening Gladys stood in the doorway and tried to drag in reluctant teams. When the reputation of the inn was established, more often than not the courtyard was filled with six or seven teams of mules, and the upper and lower floors, which between them contained three *k'angs*, were packed with bodies; but in the early weeks practically all their clients were hauled into the courtyard by Gladys.

Learning the Chinese language was also, she discovered, a slow business, but Yang was a willing teacher. He led her around the kitchen identifying articles by their Chinese names and making her repeat them after him. Poker, chopsticks, fire, pot, eggs. He had volunteered to become cook to Jeannie Lawson in the first place because he had heard of this Christian gospel, and he wished to know more about it.

Very often, now that the local inhabitants had stopped throwing earth clods at them, they ventured outside the city boundaries, walking along the mountain tracks to the isolated villages which lay within a few miles of Yangcheng. As they entered the gates of a new village they were invariably greeted with jeers and shaken fists. Although Gladys was nervous at first, under the iron tutelage of Jeannie Lawson she soon became accustomed to this reception. She also knew that, once the villagers had failed in their effort to drive away the "foreign devils," their natural curiosity would get the best of them and they would gather around and listen while Jeannie Lawson talked. Often, after a few minutes the women would become so intrigued that they would ask them all sorts of questions, staring with awe at the large, unbound feet and strange skins of their visitors. Hour after hour, day after day, Gladys practiced her Chinese. There was no alternative; only Mrs. Lawson spoke English, and the daily business of living had to be carried on in the Yang-cheng dialect. She learned some of the Bible stories in Chinese by heart, and helped from time to time at the evening storytelling. Even Yang insisted on taking a turn, although at first he was inclined to get his religious relationships confused. On two occasions, they discovered him describing enthusiastically how Jesus Christ put all his animals aboard the Ark and sailed to safety across the flood waters to Bethlehem!

Gladys was happy, even though at times Jeannie Lawson, hotblooded, dogmatic, and getting on in years, was a little difficult to live with, and inclined, in the manner of old people, to be assertive and demanding. For Gladys, just to live and be able to work in Yangcheng was enough. She realized now how circumscribed her life in England had been. In Edmonton she could see only as far as the end of the street; in Belgrave Square she was confined eternally to "servants' quarters" in a rigid caste system. No such thing existed in China.

In the immense terrain of China, expanses which reached north, south, east and west, across thousands of miles of alien culture, the faith in which she believed seemed clearer and more forceful than ever. There was a clarity, a need, an urgency in this country, where the spring sun flushed the snow down the rocky gullies in rushing torrents, where the mountains were barren, yet in the cracks and niches in the small villages there was a wealth of green and growing things. And where the mountains were not barren stretched the "loess" lands, soft, rich earth in which grew wheat and corn and millet. In the mountains the peasants terraced their plots, hoarded the precious soil, offered up prayers to the gods of wind and rain and sun so that they would be gentle and the crops would prosper. In the spring, in these latitudes, there was an ache in the air—mountain air, clean, fresh and soft, and redolent with the scent of flowers and wild roses.

She began also to understand the muleteers, the carriers and coolies. Over the flinty, narrow trail which curved and climbed through the mountains, they led their mules, laden with coal and raw cotton and pots and iron goods. The coolies bent under shoulder poles which supported fifty pounds dead weight in grain at either end. (Mules did not carry grain, because they made it smell.) They were human links of communication and transport with a heritage that stretched back to the beginnings of industry. They had dark, tanned faces, shocks of blue-black hair, narrow slitted eyes. Many of them were tall, like most northern Chinese, and sinewy and strong. Their knowledge of mules and mountains was infinite, of the world and its ways, infinitesimal. Yet they were contented, simple people. At the end of the day a bowl of food, a place on the warm brick bed, were all they desired. After six weeks' or three months' traveling, they returned to a wife, children, and a small home at one end of the trail. Often they stayed there for several weeks and helped with the harvest. Often they had families at both ends of the trail. Two wives, two sets of children, two homes, was the normal domestic situation of the average muleteer. Very often one wife would send a small gift along the old mule track with her husband to the other—perhaps a gift

Gladys Aylward shortly after her arrival in China.

Gladys Aylward with Mrs. Jeannie Lawson.

This photograph reached England after Jeannie Lawson's death. Gladys with some of her converts at prayers over Mrs. Lawson's coffin. *Back row:* Muleteers who visited the Inn of Eight Happinesses.

for a newly-born child. But they never met. The mountains separated them.

In Yangcheng Gladys found life an immense and endless adventure. The pastoral mountain background was so broad and vivid, and she was not merely an observer, an interested traveler passing across an alien landscape, but an integral part of the whole. This realization was a source of endless satisfaction to her. Until Jeannie Lawson quarreled with her, she was fully and completely absorbed with her way of living.

The quarrel was absurd, no more than a slight difference of opinion, but its results were unforeseeable. By now, after nearly eight months at the Inn of Eight Happinesses, Gladys was accustomed to Jeannie's quick outbursts of anger. Usually she could circumvent them, keeping out of the way until they had boiled over and evaporated. Jeannie liked to go for a walk every afternoon; more often than not Gladys went with her. But she was trying desperately to become proficient in the Chinese language; she spent several hours a day trying to memorize sentences and words she had written phonetically in a notebook. On this occasion, when Jeannie Lawson asked her to come for a walk, Gladys begged to be excused; she wanted to go on studying Chinese. Mrs. Lawson flew into a rage. Gladys could not calm her. She tried to explain that all she wanted to do was to understand more Chinese; if only she could learn the language, she could be of more use to Mrs. Lawson, more help at the inn.

Jeannie was not listening. With uncompromising suddenness her temper rose to boiling point. The harsh words came out in a torrent. If Gladys couldn't bother to come for a walk, then she needn't bother to stay there. As far as she was concerned, Gladys could leave, and the sooner the better. In fact she could leave right that minute. Indeed, she would help her to leave. She stormed out and returned with an armful of Gladys's possessions which she proceeded to throw at her. Weeping, Gladys fled to Yang and hid in his kitchen. Together they crouched there and listened to the tirade, while odd garments were flung down into the courtyard. Yang was very much concerned. Like all Chinese, he respected old age, and Jeannie Lawson was most certainly old enough to receive ancestral treatment.

"Perhaps it is better you do as she demands," he advised anxiously. "Leave us for a little while. Go back to Tsechow and visit the Mission there. Those ladies will be glad to give you a little holiday. Stay there for a time and then return. She will send for you after a day or two—of that I am certain. The old one will have forgotten her rage and we shall all be happy again."

"But how can I get there?" sobbed Gladys. "It's two days' journey. I can't walk all that distance."

"I will arrange with a friend of mine to provide a mule and a man to go with you," said Yang.

"But supposing I never come back?"

At that moment one of her own battered suitcases flew over the balustrade and skidded along the courtyard.

Yang spread his hands. "We both understand the honorable old one," he said gently. "She will forget and forgive. She likes you and she needs you. Perhaps it is better you make her feel that you are necessary. . . ." His shoulders lifted and his eyes were speculative.

"All right," said Gladys miserably. "I'll go."

The shudder of a heavily-slammed door overhead meant that Jeannie Lawson had retired to her room. It was Gladys's opportunity. She rescued the suitcase and packed her few things into it. Yang carried it to the gate with her and down the street to his friend who owned a mule. For a few *cash* the bargain was struck. Still weeping, Gladys hoisted herself aboard the mule.

It was a sad journey. Not even old Mrs. Smith at the Tsechow mission could cheer her up.

"We all know Jeannie," she said. "She flies off the handle for a day or two, then the whole thing is forgotten. You have a nice little holiday here, my dear, and then go back, and you mark my words, Jeannie will be overjoyed to see you."

"But what if she won't have me back?" said Gladys, voicing her deepest and most secret dread. "I've no money. I'm stuck here in the middle of China and I don't want to go home. I just can't go back to England."

"Now don't worry, dear," said Mrs. Smith soothingly. "Everything will turn out all right. Just don't worry your head. We know Jeannie. She might even send a messenger for you."

Her prophecy was accurate. Three days later, in the early morning, a messenger did arrive but from the Tsechow *yamen*. He gabbled excitedly to Mrs. Smith; Gladys could see her brow furrow as she listened. She looked a little agitated. "The story seems quite silly," she said, "but it looks as if Jeannie's had an accident."

A premonition of disaster overwhelmed Gladys. "What does he say?"

"He says that Jeannie Lawson is somewhere on the road, and—and—"

"And what?" cried Gladys in a voice full of apprehension.

"That she's dying," concluded Mrs. Smith. "Really, I don't know what to make of this."

"But where?" cried Gladys, distraught. "Where is she? I must go to her."

In quick phrases Mrs. Smith cross-examined the man. He

shrugged his shoulders. He was simply repeating something that had been passed forward by relays of disinterested and not very accurate messengers.

Gladys was in tears. "It's my fault," she wept. "I shouldn't have left her! I must go back at once!"

"Now, don't upset yourself, my dear," said Mrs. Smith gently. "We'll get you a mule and someone to go with you, and you can go off and find her at once. I'm sure she'll be all right. I know from experience how distorted these messages can become."

Gladys spent that night at the village of Chowtsun. From the garbled report which had reached Tsechow, she knew that Jeannie Lawson had left Yangcheng and gone into the mountains. It was no use, therefore, returning to that city, so she and the muleteer took a side trail, detouring through walled villages, asking everywhere for news of the old lady. No one had any word of her. On the fourth day, it was getting dark and they were approaching the small walled town of Chin Shui. They had made a wide circle around Yangcheng and were now returning to the main mule trail farther on. They passed a man leaving the city and repeated the question they had asked a hundred times. Yes, indeed he had heard of this old foreign one. She was lying very ill in Chin Shui at an inn. She was probably already dead, but they would still find her body if they hurried.

They pushed quickly on into the city. They had no trouble finding the inn where the "foreign devil" lay. It was current gossip among the townspeople. They passed through the outer door, and there in the open courtyard under the balcony they found Jeannie Lawson. The sight of her horrified Gladys. She was lying near a heap of coal against a wall. She was black with blood and coal dust, and at first Gladys thought she was dead. But when she ran to her, cry-

68

ing, "Jeannie, Jeannie!" Mrs. Lawson turned her head slightly. Her lips moved. "Is that you, Gladys?" she whispered. "Thank God you've come."

Tears streamed down the girl's face as she tried to make her more comfortable. It was almost dark. She stood up and shouted imperiously. "Bring lanterns so I can see. Bring lanterns at once! Do you hear!"

The servants of the inn came scurrying at the scolding of this second "foreign devil." The globes of lighted paper lanterns went bobbing through the darkness. They brought hot water. Gladys bathed Jeannie's open cuts and, little by little, learned the story from the half-delirious woman. The day after Gladys's departure, apparently still in her temper, she had left the inn at Yangcheng in the care of the cook, hired a mule and set off westward. She had arrived at Chin Shui and taken an upstairs room at this inn. In the darkness she had walked out onto the balcony and shouted down to the cook to make her some scrambled eggs. She had put out her hand to lean on the balustrade which in Yangcheng fenced off the upper balcony. But here there was no balustrade; it had rotted away long ago. Losing her balance, she had pitched forward and downward, crashing heavily onto the pile of coal twenty feet below.

As Gladys bathed and bandaged her cuts with pieces torn off her underclothes, she realized how badly Jeannie was injured. She seemed to have broken the fingers of both hands. Her face and body were badly skinned and coal grit was embedded in all the cuts and grazes. What was far worse, however, was the fact that she appeared to have injured her spine, for the slightest movement racked her with pain. Her scream as she fell had brought the Chinese in the inn running to her assistance. They had lifted her off the heap of coal and placed her under the veranda. They did not know what else to do, and the old lady, dazed with shock and pain, could not tell them. Then, too, the Chinese were scared of the "old one with the white hair." They were quite certain she would die within a few hours, so they left her alone. From time to time they gave her water, but not food. What was the use of wasting food on a dying "foreign devil"? Besides she didn't want any; she was quite delirious.

That she was dying, Gladys also was prepared to believe, but she did everything she could to make her more comfortable. The nearest European doctor was six days' journey away at Luan, and in Jeannie Lawson's condition and at her age it was unthinkable that she could stand such a journey.

For six weeks Gladys stayed at the inn, scarcely leaving Jeannie alone for a minute. Her condition hardly seemed to improve at all. The wounds healed, but she was still in pain, and at times mentally confused. At the end of six weeks Gladys decided that somehow or other she *had* to get her to the hospital at Luan. Unless she managed this, Jeannie would never get well. With the help of the cook and a local merchant, she rented two mules and secured a thick quilt between them. She packed it with straw, and put bedding on top. It made a comfortable litter. With an attendant muleteer, she said good-by to the friends she had made at Chin Shui and set off on the long journey to Luan.

They spent the next two evenings at Chinese inns on the mule trail. Then they came to Yangcheng, and they found that Yang was still managing the Inn of Eight Happinesses with success.

Yang accepted Mrs. Lawson's condition with a fatalism which was typical of the Chinese. The gods had willed it so. She would soon be at peace with her honorable ancestors. He was perfectly happy to go on running the inn until Gladys returned.

When they reached Luan, traveling in the same laborious manner, Jeannie Lawson was admitted to the hospital at once. There was an English doctor working in the wards, and two British nursing sisters. For four weeks more Gladys stayed with Jeannie, living in a room at the hospital.

The doctor was quite frank with her. "She has injured her spine, I'm afraid, and there is little we can do for her," he said. "She's seventy-four years old. The shock of the fall and the injury have unbalanced her mind. She'll have periods of coherence, but slowly she will become more and more paralyzed and then she will die. We don't quite know when. A few weeks, a couple of months? She's lived a long and useful life, and you must not grieve about it."

That afternoon Gladys sat by her friend's bedside and held her hand. It was one of Jeannie's moments of lucidity, and perhaps she divined the truth from the look of deep pity in the girl's eyes. Impulsively she whispered, "Oh, Gladys, let's go back to Yangcheng. Please take me home!"

Gladys looked down at the worn face of the woman who had befriended her, opened the gates of China to her. She must have been very pretty when she was young, Gladys thought, as she looked into the eyes which were still a deep, clear blue. All the years of her life Jeannie had spent fighting to establish the word of her Christian God in this alien land. Her husband had died and she had been left alone, but she had still worked on. Now she was so far away from her own people that she called a tiny hilltop city in southern Shansi, "home"! She had chosen this more adventurous, this more gallant, finale, of her own free will.

"I'll take you home today, Jeannie," Gladys said gently. "I'll go and see about the mule litter now. We'll go home together." They left three hours later.

Yang was pleased to see them back. Gladys had not realized they had so many friends, as they all came around to greet her. Jeannie was happier, but her condition grew slowly worse. The slow, paralyzing decay which the doctor had predicted ran its course. Day by day she died a little.

That last night in November she raved wildly. There was a full moon and its light poured in brightly through the open window. The dipping yellow light of the lamp, fed from its castor oil reservoir, wavered uncertainly. Gladys's shadow, when she moved to tend the sick woman, was a dark spider on the walls. The old woman's face was sunken, but her lips moved, endlessly repeating in disjointed phrases the great rhetoric that had guided her life from the beginning.

"The light of the body is the eye: if therefore thine eye be single, thy whole body shall be full of light. But if thine eye be evil, thy whole body shall be full of darkness. If therefore the light that is in thee be darkness, how great is that darkness!"

Gladys went out onto the veranda and looked up at the bright, high moon sailing against the wash of clear sky. The moonlight touched the tiles of the pagodas above the city walls with brightness. It accentuated the knife-edge ridges of the far-off peaks; it lit the gauze-like wisps of mist, wreathing them in a soft radiance. She knew now that Mrs. Lawson was dying. It had been plain to Yang for several days, and through him they had ordered the plain black coffin which stood in the courtyard below. Gladys looked down at it now. How this Chinese habit of producing the coffin before life had flickered out of the corpse would have horrified her at other periods of her life. Now she accepted it as normal custom, for she had changed greatly during the short year in Shansi.

She heard Mrs. Lawson's voice suddenly soft and resigned inside the room.

"Come unto me, all ye that labor and are heavy laden, and I will give you rest. Take my yoke upon you, and learn of me; for I am meek and lowly in heart: and ye shall find rest unto your souls. For my yoke is easy and my burden is light."

Next morning, the sun rose bright in the east, and the day came down from over the mountain peaks; and at noon Jeannie Lawson died.

CHAPTER SIX

THE WEEKS FOLLOWING Jeannie Lawson's death were among the most precarious that Gladys ever experienced in China. She was saved from possible disaster by two of the unlikeliest people: a cook and a Mandarin. Yang laid Jeannie into her coffin and sealed her down, and because it was a solemn and reverent occasion, he induced an old man of the city who owned a plate camera to come and take a picture. In the courtyard, with the muleteers and neighbors and the converts and a few odd children all anxious to have their photographs taken, they assembled decorously around the coffin of the "old one," and the shutter clicked. The old man hurried away to develop the picture. That it is reproduced in this book today is due to the fact that Gladys sent it home to her mother in Edmonton, for had she kept it, it would certainly have been lost forever.

Then she discussed their financial position with Yang. Their rent was paid for a year. The few *cash* they earned from the muleteers just about covered their overhead, but there was no margin of profit and hardly a livelihood. Still, the Mission was in being and Gladys had no intention of abandoning the inn until she was forced to. Her Chinese was improving daily; she was now fairly fluent in the mountain dialect of the Yangcheng district. Each district around had its own dialect. Villagers living twenty miles from each other in the mountains often could not understand each others' speech. They rarely moved from the place where they

74

were born; they knew nothing but their own dialect and their own folklore. In the years that followed, Gladys found it necessary to learn five distinctive dialects in that one province.

It was several weeks after Jeannie's death that Yang evolved the idea of Gladys's visiting the Mandarin of Yang-cheng to pay her respects.

"But why?" she demanded. "The Mandarin doesn't want to see me. I don't particularly want to see him. It's a waste of everybody's time."

She did not know about the complicated system of taxes, licenses and permits upon which the economy of the province was based. Jeannie Lawson's experience had protected her from this; she had performed all official duties.

"But your time of mourning is over," insisted Yang. "You should put on your best clothes and pay your respects to him. It's necessary. It is a courtesy."

"But I've never met a Mandarin in my life," protested Gladys. "I don't know what to say to him. How many times do you bow? Who speaks first? You go and find out these things and I'll consider it, but I can't afford a new robe to go in, anyway."

Yang shuffled off into the city and returned an hour later looking very crestfallen. Nobody, apparently, knew the laws governing the mode of conduct of a "foreign devil" woman when meeting a Mandarin. Everybody else, from coolie to government official, was covered by firm protocol; there were so many bows, so many obeisances. But Gladys was a strange species. Dejectedly Yang sighed, and explained that obviously a special law would have to be passed for her, and until it was, she clearly could not be granted an audience with the Mandarin. It was regrettable, but for the time being she would have to remain that unrespected and inferior being—

75

a woman. Gladys sensed his disappointment at her lack of importance.

The Mandarin of Yangcheng was a powerful figure. In that part of mountainous southern Shansi, the principal city was Tsechow. Several days' journey away, circling out from the capital, were the four smaller sister cities: Yangcheng, Chin Shui, Kaoping and Lingchuang, tiny walled citadels nestling among the high mountains. The Mandarin of Yangcheng ruled his city and district by decree from the governor and war lord at Taiyuan, the capital of Shansi far to the north. The government at Taiyuan owed nominal allegiance to the Nationalists. Yangcheng lay deep in the mountains. News traveled only as fast as a man could walk. The Mandarin commanded the power of freedom or imprisonment, life and death, over all his subjects in his territory. In a feudal society, he was an absolute lord, treated with obeisance. That he should make the first move toward the strange woman who had elected to live under his authority was, therefore, all the more surprising.

Gladys was busy upstairs when she heard the commotion down in the courtyard. She looked over the balustrade to see Yang running for the outer door. At the gate he turned and shouted up to her:

"The Mandarin's coming! The Mandarin's coming!" He sounded frightened; she saw his pigtail swing as he disappeared through the gate; and it was the last she saw of him for three hours, for although Yang had been insistent that she should meet the Mandarin, his own courage failed him completely when it came to the act.

Gladys patted her bun into place at the back of her head, and quickly smoothed her rather grubby blouse into place. It was awkward that he should catch her like this, quite unprepared, but it was his own fault if he didn't give her proper notice.

She ran down the stairs and into the courtyard just as the retinue began to troop in. It was so magnificent that she halted in mid-stride, frozen with a mixture of awe and delight. Coolies bore the sedan chair, curtained against prying eyes. Around it were grouped the Mandarin's clerks in robes of dark blue, while gathered at a respectful distance were other retainers; a backdrop of impressive, learned-looking gentlemen with pale, ivory faces, tight skull caps and black, almond eyes.

A clerk stepped forward and carefully opened the door of the chair, his arm proffered to help the Mandarin out. Gladys's eyes were round as she stared at him. He was magnificent! Tall, with black hair, a pale, ivory face, and a mustache which drooped at the corners. His wide-sleeved gown fell smoothly to pointed black shoes; his long, glossy queue hung down his back.

His eyes caught hers and she bowed. He stood looking down at her with a faintly worried expression on his face, his retainers grouped behind him. As there appeared to be no possible topic of conversation, Gladys decided the best thing to do was to make another deep bow.

"I come to ask your advice," he said at last.

"Oh!" said Gladys, so stupefied by his appearance she could think of nothing else to say.

"You are aware that for many generations the custom of footbinding has been practiced in this province?" he went on.

"Has it?" she murmured. His Chinese was pure and beautiful, flowery. She felt pleased with herself that she had no difficulty in understanding him.

77

"The feet of females are bound soon after they are born," he said.

"Oh!" said Gladys again. She realized that she was not taking a very impressive part in the conversation; she knew a little about the custom of footbinding, but as she had no idea of the point of this discussion, she did not quite know how to react.

"Now we have received a decree from the Central Government that all footbinding must cease immediately," he said.

"Have you?"

"Every woman in this province has bound feet. Therefore, someone with big feet, unbound feet, must undertake the work of inspection."

With a sudden twinge of alarm, Gladys looked down at her own size threes. In England they were reckoned small; here they were very large.

"Obviously, no man can undertake this work. It must be a woman. You have friends in the outside provinces who would know of such a woman. Will you write to them and ask them if they could send such a woman for this purpose?"

"I will do that with pleasure," said Gladys automatically. There was a momentary flutter of uneasiness as she realized that, with the exception of Mrs. Smith at Tsechow, she did not know anyone else in all China, but she hoped that thought did not show on her face.

"It is not a well-paid position," explained the Mandarin. "The wages will be one measure of millet a day and three *cash* to buy vegetables. A mule will be supplied to make the journey out to the lonely villages, and a guard of two soldiers will accompany the female. You will find such a woman for me? She is most necessary."

"I will do my utmost," repeated Gladys and, deciding that convention demanded it, she bowed again. Everyone bowed to everyone else, or so it seemed to her. It was all very polite. The Mandarin got back into his sedan chair, and the deputation moved out of the courtyard. Gladys felt rather breathless. She would have been even more breathless had she been aware that she had just secured for herself the job of official foot inspector of the Yangcheng district of Shansi; had become, in fact, a humble and lowly servant of his High and Mighty Eminence, the Mandarin of Yangcheng. She was unaware that she was to attain this new rank until several weeks later. In an effort to obtain a female foot inspector she wrote letters all over China: to the Mission in Tientsin, to Luan, to Hong Kong, to Shanghai, to wherever she thought there might be a Christian community. The replies were almost identical. First, no suitable girl, with large feet, could speak the dialect; secondly, no such girl could, or would wish to, ride a mule; thirdly, she would be unable or would not wish to exist on a staple diet of millet. Girls from Hong Kong or Tientsin, or other parts of China, liked rice! There was no rice in Yangcheng or its province, and the girls, it seemed, were not prepared to face a diet of grain for all the Mandarins in Shansi.

Approximately two months later, complete with his retinue, the Mandarin swept once again into the courtyard of the Inn of Eight Happinesses. He dismounted from his sedan chair, and his followers grouped in a serious semicircle behind him.

"You have not found a woman?" he asked accusingly.

Gladys decided that this time she would omit the bowings and scrapings. "Mandarin, I am still trying," she said humbly.

The Mandarin's dark bird's wings of eyebrows contracted slightly.

"Why have you not found a girl?" he said coldly.

79

Gladys explained all the reasons put forward by the Missions. With a contemptuous flick of his fan the Mandarin silenced her. "Then it must be *you* who becomes foot inspector," he announced.

"Me!" repeated Gladys in astonishment.

"You are the only woman in the region with big feet. You must take the job!"

"But I'm a Christian . . . I'm not Chinese. I don't know anything about feet. . . ."

"It is very simple. You will travel from village to village and tell the people of the Government's decree. You will assemble the women in the center of the villages, or in their houses, and inspect their feet. If the feet of the infants are bound you will unbind them. You will report any hindrance on the part of any village Elder to me, and I will deal with it. You will be armed with my authority and report to me personally. The Central Government is most anxious to stamp out this reprehensible habit and you must start your duties at once. Do you agree?"

As he talked, Gladys's thoughts fell into place. She wondered why she hadn't thought of it before. A mule to ride to the most distant villages? A guard to protect her? It was an opportunity without parallel for her to visit every part of the province, preaching wherever she went. She did not know whether she was allowed to suggest "conditions" to the Mandarin, but decided to risk his displeasure.

"You must realize, Excellency," she said, "that if I accept this position I shall try to convert the people of this province to Christianity wherever I go!"

There was a short silence. She wondered if she had committed an unpardonable error. Then he said quietly: "I care nothing for your religion or to whom you preach. This is a matter for the conscience of each individual. But it is important that you should do this work. The Central Government is impatient!"

Gladys realized that the Central Government was probably demanding facts and figures about the incidence of footbinding from this mountain province.

She bowed low. "I am anxious to be of assistance, Mandarin," she said. "I will gladly accept the position."

As she straightened up she caught a gleam of amusement in his eyes.

"Thank you," he said. "The mule and the soldiers will be ready for you tomorrow morning and whenever you need them from now onward. I wish you good fortune."

Everyone bowed and smiled. The important "foreign devil" from across the sea had consented to act as the Mandarin's representative. A curt reply could now be dispatched to that stupid Under-Secretary back in Taiyuan. The crisis was averted. Everyone's "face" was preserved. The deputation took its leave.

Yang came out to peer with a sort of curious terror at Gladys. "You are now important," he said. "You work for the *yamen*, you are the Mandarin's personal servant." He bowed low and humbly. It was the first time Gladys had ever really impressed him.

Gladys's journeys to the distant villages did not start at once. There was a great deal of inspection to be done within Yangcheng itself and in the houses and cave dwellings outside the city walls. What Yang had implied was true. The official blessing of the *yamen*, plus the physical presence of two rather grubby soldiers, gave her an importance she had never experienced or expected. People stood up when she spoke to them. Babies' feet were unwrapped when she demanded it.

She never forgot the first village at which she arrived as

official foot inspector. It stood near a fast-running river pounding through a narrow gorge; the houses were of one story, built of rock and mud and with green tiles. Dusty little tracks connected them, and in the dark rooms the floors were of beaten earth with only the brick communal bed raised from the ground. On the rough tables stood blue patterned chinaware and the inevitable wooden chopsticks. Children were everywhere—small, grimy, noisy, quilt-padded infants, brown faced and clamorous, some still at their mothers' breasts; others were tagging around the flanks of Gladys's mule. The mountains rose steeply all around. In the settlement the plum and peach trees were in blossom and little fields of yellow mustard seed, dark green cotton, and bright green millet stalks terraced one face of the mountainside.

As soon as they had passed through the gate, villagers began to crowd around. The soldiers inquired after the village Elder. When he appeared they told him of the Mandarin's decree. He was an old, shriveled man with a thin goatee—a peasant whose experience and age had elevated him to the post which made him responsible to the Mandarin. He nodded his head seriously as he listened. The village "crier" was dispatched to tell the villagers to assemble in the square. Peasants had to be fetched from the fields, from their houses, from tending their animals. When everyone was present, the Elder informed them in a high, cracked voice that footbinding would cease from now on; that the feet of children still able to recover would be unbound. The Mandarin had given these orders. The soldiers, who thoroughly enjoyed their small authority, then reiterated the proclamation, and made it quite clear that anyone who disobeyed the order would at once be thrown into prison.

Then they turned to tell Gladys that it was time for the inspection. She did not know quite what to do, but to make some sort of move walked across the square toward the nearest small house. A crowd gathered behind her. Reassured by the raucous presence of her two soldiers, she went in through the open door. The soldiers waited outside. It was clean and neat, but there was no furniture, only a few cooking pots and utensils; the quilted bedding was piled on the brick *k'ang* where the family slept. A small, dark-eyed girl, aged about three, clung to her mother's trousers and looked nervously at Gladys. A single glance was sufficient to tell that her feet were bound.

"That one," said Gladys, trying to insert a note of authority into her voice. "Unbind her feet!"

Two women neighbors and a grandmother had now appeared in the room. The mother took the child on her lap and all four women began to undo the bandages.

To cover her own nervousness, Gladys maintained a running commentary, as each fold of cloth fell away.

"That's it. Come on, now. Hurry up! If God intended little girls to have horrible stubby little feet, he'd have made them like that in the first place, wouldn't he? Feet are to walk with, not to shuffle up and down with, aren't they? I don't care if the husbands say you should do it or not. They should try it sometime, and see if they like hobbling about on little club feet. Any man who tells you to do it goes to prison at once; that's the law now. . . ."

The last bandages dropped, revealing tiny white feet with toes bent downward and up into the soles.

"Look at those feet!" exclaimed Gladys. "How d'you expect the poor child to walk properly with those feet?"

She almost pushed the women away, and kneeling down gently pried the toes up and away from the sole. The child regarded her with wide, timid eyes.

"There," said Gladys softly. "Five little piggies all ready

to go to market." She massaged the foot tenderly. Suddenly there was a quick, liquid giggle from the child, who wriggled with delight.

The spell was broken. The women came closer, chattering happily. When she came to know them better, Gladys was to realize what an independent, courageous group these mountain women were.

"Yes, it is a good law," they said. Everyone now wanted to help in the foot massage; everyone wanted to tell of the pain and the trouble their own feet had given them for the past ten years. One of the neighbors rushed off to the next house to explain what had to be done, and the news went around the village before Gladys had finished her first chore. On her visits she soon found housewives dutifully exhibiting all their little girls with unbound feet. What part the soldiers' cheerfully repeated order, "Unbind feet or go to prison!" played in this social reform it is difficult to know, but everyone was very amiable.

Gladys stayed that night at the house of the Elder, and the rest of her journey through the villages was very much a repetition of this scene.

Many of the villages in the remote valleys were cut off almost entirely from the outside world. They raised cattle and pigs and chickens; they wore their own cotton cloth. They were self-sufficient, growing their own food, making their own clothes, with a folklore handed down to them from a thousand generations. They were simple, kindly people, possessing a cheerfulness, fortitude and calm that Gladys had never before encountered.

Her visits became events of considerable excitement; she brought news of the outside world, such as it was; and as a storyteller she commanded their devotion and admiration. The children clamored behind her old gray mule as she jogged in through the gateway, and the soldiers shouted and waved to old friends as they made for the inn or the Elder's house where they were staying. In the evenings the villagers crowded in to learn the new songs which swung along with a lilt and intonation quite different from their own, and listened to the stories Gladys told of a man called Jesus Christ whose honorable ancestor was the great God who lived in the clouds high above. It appeared to them that this man Jesus had lived in a simple society closely akin to their own. He had encountered much the same problems as they did. He had obeyed roughly the same rules of civilized conduct as they did. He was an enthralling person, and the official foot inspector's supply of stories seemed inexhaustible.

These, for Gladys, were the years of endless content. With the Inn of Eight Happinesses as a base and a small Christian community growing up around it, her wanderings through the mountains were always adventures. The weeks passed into months and the months into years, and there was a harvest of happiness to be gathered from each day. Rumors of other happenings occasionally came over the mountains, brought by the muleteers, but it was news of a different world, a world too far away to matter, a world beyond the broad barrier of the Yellow River—the Hwang Ho—a world almost as far away as the moon.

In winter the frost would rime on the tiled roofs of the pagodas, the mule teams would steam as they clopped up the street; long dripping icicles hung from the gargoyles' noses on the temple roofs; and from December to March one wore trousers and coat, padded warmly with raw cotton. When the snow came howling over the mountains from the north, it packed down in drifts into the valleys and gorges, filled the streets of the city three and four feet deep. Sound was deadened; nowhere in all the hundreds of miles of the mountain country did anything move except the crashing avalanches and the snow-laden wind.

Life came to a standstill. You hibernated under a thick cocoon of snow. You sat around your *k'ang* fed by coal carried in from seams to be found everywhere on the mountain sides, mended your clothes and made new shoes and thought of what the spring might bring. You visited no one, talked little; you sat secure in your winter world with enough grain to last you out, and waited patiently for the snows to pass.

And then the spring came, putting the new-old ache into bone and blood, and bringing a renewed awareness of beauty.

In this land of high mountains and deep valleys, where living was meager and hard, Gladys grew to maturity. All that had gone before was a preparation for this, and this only a preparation for what was to come. She understood here that any religion which attempted to act as a chastity belt, or which was thin, humorless and arid, would be rejected by these simple mountain folk as they had rejected every other form of invasion. The religion she preached was a simple one. It told of strength through humility, wisdom through love, and life everlasting through faith.

There arrived during her second year at Yangcheng a pleasant young man called Lu Yung-cheng. He was a convert sent from Tsechow by Mrs. Smith, who said she would pay his salary, amounting to ninepence a month. He was useful if only because he could keep an ear to Yang's romantic interpretation of the Scriptures. It was about two weeks after he arrived that he and Gladys were standing in the courtyard when the messenger from the *yamen* rushed in waving a piece of scarlet paper. He gabbled at such a rate that Gladys found it difficult to understand him.

"What's the paper for, anyway?" she asked Lu Yung-cheng.

86

"It's an official summons from the *yamen*," said Lu Yung-cheng, nervously. "A riot has broken out in the men's prison."

Gladys was not much concerned. "Oh, has it?" she said.

"You must come at once," said the messenger urgently. "It is most important!"

Gladys stared at him: "But what's the riot in the prison got to do with us? It can't have anything to do with my foot inspection."

"You must come at once!" reiterated the messenger loudly. "It is an official order." He hopped from one foot to the other in impatience.

Lu Yung-cheng looked at her doubtfully. "When that piece of red paper arrives from the *yamen*, you must go." There was a nervous tremor in his voice.

"All right, *you* go and see what it's all about," said Gladys. "It's obviously a man's job. I know nothing about prisons. I've never been in one in my life. Though I really don't see what you're supposed to do."

She could see from Lu Yung-cheng's face that the prospect did not appeal to him. "Hurry, please hurry!" cried the messenger. Reluctantly, Lu Yung-cheng trailed after him to the door. Gladys watched him reach the opening, take a quick look behind at her, then dodge swiftly to the left as the messenger turned to the right. She could hear the sound of his running feet as he tore down the road. Within two seconds the messenger discovered his loss. He stormed back through the doorway crying, 'Ai-ee-ee!" and shaking his fist in rage. He raced across the courtyard toward Gladys, a little fat man without dignity.

"Now *you* must come," he shouted. "This is an official paper. You are ordered to come. You *must* come. Now! With me! If you refuse, you will get into trouble!"

87

"All right," she said mildly. "I'll come. I really don't know what's the matter with Lu Yung-cheng. He must feel ill or something. But I certainly don't see what a riot in the prison has to do with me. . . ."

They hurried up the road and in through the East Gate. A few yards inside the gate the blank outside wall of the prison flanked the main street. From the other side came an unholy noise: screams, shouts, yells, the most horrible sounds.

"My goodness," said Gladys, "it certainly is a riot, isn't it?"

The governor of the prison, small, pale-faced, his mouth set into a worried line, met her at the entrance. Behind were grouped half a dozen of his staff.

"We are glad you have come," he said quickly. "There is a riot in the prison; the convicts are killing each other."

"So I can hear," she said. "But what am I here for? I'm only the missionary woman. Why don't you send the soldiers in to stop it?"

"The convicts are murderers, bandits, thieves," said the governor, his voice trembling. "The soldiers are frightened. There are not enough of them."

"I'm sorry to hear that," said Gladys. "But what do you expect me to do about it? I don't even know why you asked me to come. . . ."

The governor took a step forward. "You must go in and stop the fighting!"

"I must go in! Are you mad? If I went in they'd kill me!"

The governor's eyes were fixed on her with hypnotic urgency. "But how can they kill you? You have been telling everybody that you have come here because you have the living God inside you. . . ."

Gladys felt a small, cold shiver down her back. When she swallowed, her throat seemed to have a gritty texture.

"The—living God?" she stammered.

"You preach it everywhere, in the streets and villages. If you preach the truth—if your God protects you from harm— then you can stop this riot." She stared at him. Her mind raced around in bewilderment, searching for some fact that would explain her beliefs to this simple, deluded man. A little cell in her mind kept blinking on and off with an urgent semaphore message: "It's true! You have been preaching that your Christian God protects you from harm. Fail now, and you are finished in Yangcheng. Abandon your faith now, and you abandon it forever!" It was a desperate challenge. Somehow, she had to maintain face. Oh, these stupidly simple people! But how could she go into the prison with those men—murderers, thieves, bandits—rioting and killing each other inside those walls! By the sounds, louder now, a small human hell had broken loose. How *could* she? "I must try," she said to herself. "I must try. Oh, God, give me strength."

She looked up at the governor's pale face, knowing that now hers was the same color. "All right," she said. "Open the door. I'll go in to them." She did not trust her voice to say any more.

"The key!" snapped the governor. "The key, quickly."

One of his orderlies came forward with a huge iron key. It looked designed to unlock the deepest, darkest dungeon in the world. In the keyhole the giant wards grated loudly; the immense iron-barred door swung open. Literally she was pushed inside. It was dark. The door closed behind her. She heard the great key turn. She was locked in the prison with a horde of raving criminals who by their din sounded as if they had all gone insane. A dark tunnel, twenty yards long, stretched before her. At the far end it appeared to open out into a courtyard. She could see figures racing across the entrance. With faltering footsteps, she walked through it and came to an abrupt standstill, rooted in horror.

The courtyard was about sixty feet square, with queer cage-like structures around all four sides. Within its confines a writhing, fiendish battle was going on. Several bodies were stretched out on the flagstones. One man, obviously dead, lay only a few feet from her, blood still pouring from a great wound in his scalp. There was blood everywhere. Inside the cage-like structures small private battles were being fought. The main group of men, however, were watching one convict who brandished a large, bloodstained chopper. As she stared, he suddenly rushed at them and they scattered wildly to every part of the square. The man on the ground with the gash in his skull obviously hadn't run fast enough.

No one took any notice whatsoever of Gladys. For fully half a minute she stood motionless with no idea what to do. The man rushed again; the group parted; he singled one man out and chased him. The man ran toward Gladys, then ducked away. The madman with the axe halted only a few feet from her. Without any plan, hardly realizing what she was doing, she instinctively took two angry steps toward him.

"Give me that chopper," she said furiously. "Give it to me at once!"

The man looked at her. For three long seconds the wild, dark pupils, staring from bloodshot eyes, glared at her. He took two paces forward. Then suddenly, meekly, he held out the axe. Quickly she snatched the weapon from his hand and held it rigidly by her side. She was conscious that there was blood on the blade and that it would stain her trousers. The other convicts—there must have been fifty or sixty men—stared from every corner of the courtyard. All action was frozen in that one moment of intense drama, and she knew that she must somehow clinch her psychological advantage.

"All of you!" she shouted. "Come over here. Come on, form into a line!" She realized that the voice belonged to her, but she had never heard it so shrill. She screamed at them, gabbled at them like an undersized, infuriated sergeant, like a schoolmarm with a class of naughty children. "Get into line at once. You, over there! Come on, line up in front of me!"

Obediently the convicts shambled over, forming into a ragged group before her. She regarded them stormily, there was silence, and suddenly her fear had gone. In its place was an immense, profound pity. They were so wretched. They were so hopeless. A mass of thin faces: angular cheekbones, puckered lips; faces contorted with misery, pain and hunger. Eyes dark with fear and despair looked into hers. These men were remnants of humanity, half creatures dressed in rags, caked in dust, running with lice; animals more than men, and the cages in which they were penned around the arena were those of brutes. She could have wept openly that human creatures could be so wretched. With an effort, she took command again. The fear had gone, yes, but she knew she must still control them with her authority.

"You should be ashamed of yourselves," she said, berating them again like an angry mother scolding a crowd of naughty children. "All this noise and all this mess!" Mess! She waved her arms to indicate the bodies and blood the battle had left behind. "The governor sent me in here to find out what it was all about. Now, if you clean up this courtyard and promise to behave in future, I'll ask him to deal leniently with you this time." She tried to keep her eyes away from the still figures of the dead. She knew she must focus their attention until all the desperate violence had seeped away. "Now, what is your grievance?" she snapped. "Why did you start fighting like this?"

There was no answer. Several hung their heads in shame.

"I want you to appoint a spokesman," she went on. "He can tell me what the trouble is. And then you can start cleaning up this courtyard at once. Now go over in that corner and appoint your spokesman. I'll wait here."

The convicts trooped over into the corner she indicated and talked among themselves. A few moments later, one of the taller men, of slightly better physique, approached. Like the others, he was dressed in rags.

"My name is Feng," he said. "I am their spokesman."

While the others swabbed up the blood with rags, and moved the dead bodies into less spectacular positions, Gladys listened to his story. Later she learned that he had once been a Buddhist priest; he had been convicted of theft from the other priests of the temple and sentenced to eight years in jail. He explained that no one really knew why, or how, the riot had started. They were allowed the chopper—he indicated the axe which Gladys still carried—for an hour every day to cut up their food. Someone had quarreled over its possession, someone else had joined in, and suddenly, without anyone knowing exactly why, the volcano of passion had erupted and a lava of blood flowed everywhere. He could not explain this strange occurrence. Perhaps it was that many of the men had been there for many years, he said. Unless their friends or relatives sent in food, they starved. It was hard to sit up against a wall and starve to death while other men ate. Sometimes the officials took one of their number out into the square and executed him. That terror hung over many heads. He could not explain the outbreak, but the walls were high and the doors were strong; they never saw the outside world, women, or the mountains, a tree in blossom or a friendly face. Sometimes the spirit grew so oppressed that it burst out of a man in a wild tumult of violence. That, he thought, is what had occurred. They were all very sorry.

"What do you do all day in here?" asked Gladys seriously.

"Do? There is nothing to do."

"No occupation of any sort?"

"None!"

"But a man must have work, something to do. I shall see the governor about it."

It was at that moment she became conscious that the governor and his retinue were behind her. She did not find out until later that there was a small opening toward the end of the tunnel through which they had heard everything. The noise of the riot had died and they had now thought it safe to enter and take an official part in the peace treaty.

The governor bowed to Gladys.

"You have done well," he said gratefully. "We must thank you."

"It's disgraceful," she said bitterly. "These men are locked up here week after week, year after year, with nothing to do. Nothing to do at all!"

"I do not understand." The governor's bewilderment was rather ludicrous. Gladys could, however, sense his gratitude and decided to press her point. "Of course you have riots if they've nothing to occupy their time, year after year. You must find them occupations."

The governor was still completely puzzled. "Occupations?" he repeated.

"They must have work to do. We must get looms so they can weave cloth. We must find them jobs so that they can earn a little money and buy food, and get back a little self-respect."

93

The governor nodded. Whether he agreed or not, she could not tell. "We will discuss it later," he said amiably.

"I have promised them there will be no reprisals," she said. The governor nodded again. A few corpses were rarely the subject of an official inquiry, or even an embarrassment to the Chinese penal system. "As long as there is no repetition," he said, "we shall forget all about it."

"That is good," said Gladys. She turned to Feng. "I'm going now, but I shall come back. I promised I will do all I can to help you."

She saw upon her the dark eyes of the priest who was a thief. "Thank you," he said. "Thank you, Ai-weh-deh."

She did not know at the time what the word "Ai-weh-deh" meant. That evening she asked Lu Yung-cheng when he returned from the long walk he had so suddenly decided to take.

"Ai-weh-deh?" he said, interestedly. "It means 'the Virtuous One.' "

She was known as Ai-weh-deh for all her remaining years in China.

The Small Woman

CHAPTER SEVEN

THE EPISODE in the prison raised Gladys's prestige considerably in Yangcheng. Becoming official foot inspector had given her some importance, but stopping a jail riot had conferred honor of a different sort altogether. She noticed that merchants, standing in their shop doorways, who had ignored her for so long, now bowed politely as she passed. Her two soldiers were as pleased about the affair as if they had received a raise in pay. She had gained much "face."

She did not forget her promise to the prisoners, either. The governor was an educated man, and, at heart, kindly. In the years that followed he became her good friend. If the condition of his prison was abysmal, it was because the conditions in all Chinese prisons were dreadful. If only to stop riots from breaking out, he was perfectly willing to accept suggestions from Gladys. No large-scale reforms could be accomplished; there was no money in the *yamen* funds allotted to the improvement of prisons. Gladys had no money either, but she did manage to get a couple of old looms from friends of the governor, and a supply of yarn. She obtained cotton cloth and set them to making the puttees which were worn in Shansi, and a miller's wheel so they could grind grain and make a few *cash* out of that work. She visited the prisoners regularly —almost every day when she was in Yangcheng. She taught them facts about hygiene, and read them stories. She managed to get some domesticated rabbits and they kept these in hutches and bred them. But perhaps her greatest triumph came when

95

the governor's old school friend, a scholar of some repute visited Yangcheng.

"He is a Christian," said the governor, importantly. "Perhaps I could prevail upon him to preach in your Mission."

"A good idea," said Gladys at once. "And I'll tell you what. Why don't we have all your convicts down to listen to him?"

The governor was perturbed. "That is impossible!"

"Why is it impossible? Some of them have never left that courtyard for ten years or more. It would be a great event for them. Do them all good!"

"But they're convicts!"

"You could guard them. It would flatter your old friend, too . . . if he's a good Christian, that is."

From the moment Gladys stopped the riot in his jail, the governor had regarded her with some awe. At least, on that occasion, *her* religion had worked, whereas his had not. Reluctantly, after a little more persuasion, he agreed to let them out for this one occasion.

Gladys never forgot the Sunday the convicts came to church. Manacled together with heavy chains, they were marched down the main streets and out of the West Gate. The people lined the roads to stare at them. Outside the gate, the whole troop halted instinctively and stared at the mountains. For two whole minutes the soldiers who were guarding them allowed them to stand murmuring together, and look out at freedom. Then they marched down the narrow street to the Inn of Eight Happinesses, filed through the courtyard, and into the old ancestral hall at the far end, which had now been converted into a mission hall.

They sat on the floor while the portly, beaming friend of the governor preached to them for three long hours. It was perhaps the most blissful church service ever conducted in the province of Shansi. At the end of it, through their spokesman,

Town Crier calling villagers to the West Gate of Yangcheng.

A woman with bandaged feet. It was Gladys Aylward's duty as foot inspector in southern Shansi to break down this centuries-old custom.

Ai. Ai. Ninepence says not ca
that, she nice old lady, so
you know what I am in the
of a child of 8.
    Life is pitiful, death so fam
suffering + pain so common, y
would not be anywhere else
Do not wish me out of this
any way seek to get me out, I
will not be got out while thi
trial is on, These are my peop
God have given them to me, +
live or die with them for Him a
His glory.

Photos John R. Freeman &

Gladys Aylward's certificate of Chinese naturalization, 1936.

Part of a letter from Ai-weh-deh to her parents in Edmonton.

they thanked Gladys gravely for allowing them this privilege, and with chains jangling marched back to jail.

It was also in her second year at Yangcheng that she had her first small altercation with the Mandarin. She had just returned from a foot-inspection tour into the mountains, and was walking down the main street rehearsing the speech she was going to make to him. As her employer, she decided he should know about certain things and put a stop to them.

"Mandarin," she was going to say, with reluctance but with some primness, "I wish to discuss with you the status of women." She would pause to let that point sink in. "Is it right," she would continue, "that a man is allowed to beat his wife? Is it right that a husband has the power to sell his wife, even to kill his wife? These things have been brought forcibly to the notice of your most loyal and obedient employee, in her journeys into the mountain villages. Respectfully, I would like to know what you intend to do about these matters? I know they are of immemorial origin, but that does not make them any less repellent."

She halted in mid-thought when she saw the woman sitting on the pavement with her feet in the roadway. The woman was swarthy, coarse, dirty. Heavy silver earrings dangled from her earlobes. Silver and jade pins were stuck in her hair; she wore a silver necklace and embossed bracelets; her baggy trousers were secured at the ankle by bright green puttees. The puttees first attracted Gladys's attention. Although they were a normal part of Shansi dress, she had never seen them of that color before; the woman must come from a village which she had never visited or even heard about. Gladys walked toward her intending to find the answer to these questions.

As she approached she saw that a child leaned against the woman's knee. An appalling, sickly scrap of a child, clad in a dirty bit of loincloth, it had legs like stalks, its belly was swollen with malnutrition, and its head and body were covered with running sores. The child's condition made it impossible even to tell its sex. The questions were forgotten, as she stared in horror.

"Woman, you have no right to sit on the side of the road with a child in that condition," she said sternly.

The woman's dark eyes flicked up at her insolently. "Mind your own business," she cried.

"It *is* my business," said Gladys indignantly, remembering her official status as foot inspector. "You let the baking sun pour on the child's head much longer, and it will die!"

"What has it got to do with you whether it dies or not?" sneered the woman. "If it does, I'll soon get another one."

Gladys glared down at her. She guessed from her manner that the woman was not the child's mother. She remembered vaguely that she had heard about people like this. Child dealers? That was it—people who bought and sold children. In the Shansi mountains they were thought of as devils, mentioned only in whispers.

The woman's next remark confirmed her thoughts. She said provocatively: "Would you like it? You can have it for two dollars."

Gladys realized at once that, as current market prices went, the price was cheap. A pretty girl, suitable as a bride, would cost ninety dollars at least; even a young female child would fetch ten dollars. But who would want this sick and weakly infant?

"I haven't got two dollars," Gladys retorted. "It's sick and likely to die, and it will take two more dollars to bury it; and that makes four dollars."

The woman pulled a face. Her eyes were hard. "You can have it for a dollar and a half, then."

"I haven't got a dollar and a half, and I don't want the child, anyway."

She walked away, the woman's jeering laughter following her. No one else passing along the street had bothered to listen to their conversation. But, as she walked toward the *yamen*, a surge of indignation began to rise inside her, indignation which did not lessen even though, as usual, it was an hour before she was granted an audience with the Mandarin. By the time the gong boomed, and the soldier pushed open the great door to admit her into the presence, she was aching to tell him about the child-dealer. She knew, however, that you could not immediately protest to a Mandarin, no matter how serious your complaint. Courtesies came first. She bowed low before the imperious scarlet-robed figure, obeying the ancient ritual of the small official addressing the high and mighty.

"Mandarin, are you well?" she asked.

"Yes, I am well. You are well?"

"Yes, I am well. Have you eaten your food?"

"Yes, I have eaten my food. Have you eaten your food?"

"Thank you, yes. Mandarin, are your old relations well?"

"Yes, my old ones are very well."

This went on for about a minute, and then, the courtesies over, she handed him the slip of paper containing her report. It was a very brief report, because in those early days before she had learned to write in Chinese, she had to get someone to write the Chinese characters for her. Her reports, in fact, were masterpieces of simplicity. This one read:

"Gladys Aylward has been to Chowtsun. Gladys Aylward has come back from Chowtsun." The names of the district or village might alter with each trip, but her written reports did not. All the details of her work she gave him verbally. A smile creased the Mandarin's mouth as he took the paper. Seeing him thus in his bright scarlet robes, with high collar, scarlet cap and wide, sweeping sleeves, she always took some seconds to get over her feeling of awe.

"You have things to tell me," he said.

Gladys answered: "What do you do with dealers in children?"

The dark, thin eyebrows lifted slightly. "I do not understand you."

"A few yards away from this *yamen*, a woman tried to sell me a child for two dollars. What do you do about that?"

Gladys intuitively knew that her question worried him. He walked to the end of the chamber and back before replying. Then he said: "You do not do anything."

"But I don't understand," said Gladys. "It's wrong!"

"If she is indeed a child-dealer, she belongs to a gang of wicked and desperate people. If you interfere with them they commit horrible crimes. It is better that you forget all about it. It has nothing to do with you."

"But, Mandarin . . ."

"Now, tell me what you have done in the district of Chowtsun."

It was a command, and Gladys summarized the women she had seen, the speeches she had made. It took half an hour. When she had finished, the Mandarin nodded his head. He picked up the small hammer and rapped the gong. It was the signal for the doors to be opened; the interview was over. As she turned to go, he stayed her with a gesture of his hand.

"About the child-dealer, the law says that Ai-weh-deh, the Virtuous One, is to put her head in the air and pass on the other side of the road. And you will not repeat my words to anyone! Go!"

The doors were open. Gladys walked toward them. She was deeply disappointed in this man for whom she felt so much respect. She turned in the doorway.

"I have to inform you, Mandarin," she said, "that I did not come to China only to observe your laws. I came for the love of Jesus Christ, and I shall act upon the principles of His teaching, no matter what you say."

It was a well-timed exit. Before the surprised Mandarin had time to reply she had gone. Months later, when they were on terms of greater intimacy, he reminded her of that meeting. He told her that his friendship and his respect for her had stemmed from that action. It was the first time in his term of office that any person, man or woman, had dared to question his authority as Mandarin. It was certainly the first time in his life that any woman had spoken to him in such a fashion.

Gladys walked swiftly down the main street. The woman was still there. When she saw Gladys she called out: "Lady with the heart of pity! Here you are again. I will sell you the child for a hundred and fifty *cash*."

Gladys stopped and stared at her. "I haven't got a hundred and fifty *cash*."

"Then how much would you give for it?"

"I haven't any money, and what would I do with the child?"

"But you do want it, don't you?"

Gladys started to dispute the remark, then suddenly stopped. She did want the child.

"How much would you give?" said the woman in a wheedling tone.

Gladys reached inside her jacket pocket. She had a few copper *cash* there, in value equal to about ninepence. She took it out.

"I'll give you this, but not a penny more."

The woman cupped her hand to take the money. "She is yours." She stood up and hurried off down the street; Gladys looked down at the child. Its age was indeterminate—roughly between four and six years old.

"Come with me!" she said. The child made no move and seemed to comprehend little. Gladys took her by the hand and led her along the main street, through the gate and back to the inn. Inside the main room the little girl ran to the darkest corner and crouched there, terrified. Gladys fetched in the cook, Yang, to see what she had brought home. He regarded the half-naked, sickly mite in silence for a few seconds.

"Well, you've done a fine thing," he said. "What d'you want such a child for? It will die very quickly."

"Give her some food," said Gladys. "The poor little thing looks nearly dead already."

Yang fetched a bowl of millet and placed it on the floor near the child, who eyed it hungrily, then rushed over, grabbed the bowl and retreated to a corner to scoop the food into her mouth with her fingers.

"We shall have trouble with this child," said Yang. Gladys noticed that at least he had said "we." That gave her a little more confidence.

Although she was christened with the Chinese name of Mei-en, Beautiful Grace, to Gladys the child's nickname was always "Ninepence." She did not learn about her past until many years later. As the months passed, she grew into a pretty little girl, full of charm and impudence. And it was through Ninepence that the family increased. One afternoon she came scurrying into the courtyard, her black eyes popping in excitement.

"Is the food ready?" she called up to Gladys, who was standing on the balcony.

"Nearly ready."

They had their own evening meal in the late afternoon, so that they could be ready for work when the muleteers arrived.

"Is it a nice meal?" asked Ninepence eagerly.

"Of course, it's nice. Isn't it always nice?" Ninepence as a rule was not concerned about food. "Go on. Run off and play. I'll call you when it's ready."

Ninepence looked up very seriously. "If I was willing to eat a little less of the meal, would you be willing to eat a little less also?"

Gladys had no idea what she was getting at. "Yes, of course."

"Then if we put the two 'lesses' in a basin, we'd have enough food for one more person, wouldn't we?"

"Ninepence," said Gladys severely, "what are you up to now?"

"Do you know," said Ninepence, frowning in concentration, "there's a little boy outside the door who hasn't even got a little 'less' in his basin?"

Gladys looked down at the small child in the middle of the large courtyard, a small blue-uniformed figure with a very serious face.

"Ninepence," she said, "if you're willing to go without, I am, too. We'll give it to this boy. Go and bring him in."

Ninepence shouted out, and a ragged little urchin about eight years old appeared from under the balcony. He was in dirty rags, a male replica of Ninepence when she first arrived. Ninepence had discovered him begging on the streets. He ate his meal with relish and stayed with them for the next ten years. His nickname thereafter was always "Less."

He was old enough to tell Gladys his story. Bandits had raided his village in Hopeh. They had killed the men and taken the women off with them. Less's mother had been pregnant. Her labor pains started on the forced march and the bandits left her behind in a ditch. How much of his mother's agony he comprehended, Gladys did not wish to think about, but he saw her die, and after tugging in vain at her clothes, left her and returned to their village. It was in ashes. Only corpses lay in the ruins. He wandered away into the mountains, begged food, joined up with the muleteers on their journeys across the trails, and eventually reached Yangcheng. There at the Inn of Eight Happinesses, he became the second child taken to the heart of Ai-weh-deh, the Virtuous One.

The third child arrived in the spring of the next year. They had gone to wash their clothes in the first warm spell of bright weather, for in the spring the whole town washed its clothes on the rocks of the river bank a few hundred yards from the East Gate. Gladys was dutifully pounding the wet, quilted garments with a piece of wood, hopeful at least that the lice would not dodge all her blows, when she heard Ninepence and Less calling behind her on the bank. She turned to look; they had a small child about two years old walking between them, holding their hands.

"Where did you find him?" called Gladys. "Take him back to where he belongs, this very minute."

"But he doesn't belong to anybody," called Ninepence. "We've looked everywhere. There's no one else around."

Gladys glared at them. "Well, maybe he's strayed from the town, then. Somebody must own him."

"Can we take him home with us?" asked Ninepence, hopefully, the real point of her anxiety now emerging.

"What!" said Gladys indignantly. "Indeed we can't! Do you think I want to be dragged up before the Mandarin for child-stealing?"

"But he really is lost," insisted Less. "We've looked everywhere."

"Wait till I've finished this washing. I'll find his parents."

But she did not find his parents. They searched along the banks and up the hillside. There were no buildings near by. They called aloud at the top of their voices. No one turned up to claim the child, and when they had done all they could they took him home with them and let him sleep at the Inn.

Afterward, even though they posted notices on the city gates, and the Mandarin sent the town crier around, no one claimed him.

So now she was responsible for three children. "Bao-Bao," Precious Bundle, had joined the family. In the years which followed, she was to become official parent to two more and unofficial mother to children without number. In 1936, when the Yellow River flooded and refugees came up into the mountains, they brought with them a small boy called Francis whom no one owned and no one wanted. And Lan Hsiang was a small girl of eight, "left over" from a law case in the Mandarin's court. She had no parents, and the Mandarin decided that it would be an excellent idea if she became a member of Gladys's family. "Haven't I got enough children?" said Gladys in some irritation. "You are the best person to look after her," said the Mandarin with the smooth Oriental authority that permitted no argument.

It was the governor of the prison who solved the problem of their schooling. He had three children, and there was no school at all in Yangcheng. Children were taught at home, if they were taught at all. "Therefore we must open a school here!" said the prison governor. "We can engage a teacher from Luan—if all the parents will make a small donation toward his salary."

So the school was started.

Five years from the time it opened Gladys discovered the story of Ninepence's past. She had grown up into a very pretty little girl, and brother Less watched over her with great concern. It was he who reported to Gladys that for two or three days in succession a man had waited outside the school for Ninepence and tried to talk to her, even tried to take her arm on one occasion. He was very worried about it.

It worried Gladys also. She told them she would meet them

at school next day, and if the man showed up Less could point him out to her. The man was there all right, and although he did not try to approach the child with Gladys present, he looked at them all with glinting, insolent eyes. Gladys didn't know what to do; so, as always in such cases, she went to see her old friend, the Mandarin.

"It is no use apprehending him unless we catch him in the act," said the Mandarin thoughtfully. "But I will have a soldier standing by outside the school every day, and if this man lays a hand on the girl again, she must scream and we will arrest him."

The man fell into the trap the very next day. He caught Ninepence by the arm as she came out through the school door and tried to drag her off with him. Less, prowling in the rear, flew at him like an enraged bulldog and buried his teeth in his arm. When the soldier ran up a few seconds later he had considerable difficulty prying Less away. The man was removed to prison.

Next day the Mandarin opened the inquiry and an interesting story was revealed. The man who was trying to kidnap Ninepence was no more than an agent for a designing uncle. So simple was his approach that the only way of taking Ninepence he could think of was to drag her off after school. It seemed that Ninepence's mother had been very happy with her husband and baby daughter. But her husband had died and her mother-in-law, not wanting a female child, had married off mother and daughter into another family. There Ninepence's mother had also died, leaving her as an unwanted female child in a household in which she had no blood relations. She had been given away, passed through many hands before the child-dealer had met Gladys in the main street of Yangcheng.

The fact that the "foreign devil" had taught Ninepence and

was looking after her quickly filtered back to the grandmother at their mountain farm in a village many miles from Yangcheng. They made no move to take her back. In China, the birth of a girl child was looked upon as a disaster, and neighbors and relatives commented acidly upon the misfortune. Unloved by everyone except the unfortunate mother, who had no rights in the matter anyway, the child was often killed at birth. If left to live, the girl would drudge and slave and be married off as soon as possible. As soon as a girl was betrothed she was regarded as belonging to another family. Who would want, therefore, to lavish love, affection or money upon a girl child who would soon belong to someone else? If a woman did not give a man a son, she was quickly discarded for a second, third, or fourth wife, who could remedy the error.

If, therefore, Ninepence's uncle had managed to spirit her away, it is doubtful whether Gladys would have found redress at law. What had happened was quite simple. Grandmother and grandfather had died leaving a farm and money, with only two people in line of inheritance: the uncle and Ninepence. What would have happened to Ninepence had she been kidnapped, it is unpleasant even to consider. But now, his design revealed, he was about to contest Gladys's claim to the child in the Mandarin's court.

The Mandarin informed Gladys of the case against her after the preliminary evidence; she would have to appear in court to defend her claim to Ninepence.

"But what can I do? I know nothing about Chinese court procedure," she protested.

The Mandarin looked very bland and impassive. "Before you speak, you will look at me," he said, urbanely. "You will say only 'Yes' or 'No.' If I shake my head slightly you will say 'No.' If I nod my head slightly you will say 'Yes.' You understand?"

"Yes, I understand, but I can't lose Ninepence now! She belongs to me. I love her. I've looked after her all these years."

"She will not be taken from you," said the Mandarin, quietly. "I am the judge in this matter, and I can promise you that. But these things must be done properly. When you are summoned, you will come to the court and do as I say."

The day of the inquiry arrived. The messenger from the *yamen* brought the red paper and Gladys went off to court. She listened to the long speeches of the lawyer appearing for the uncle. She was asked many questions herself, and looked carefully for the slight guidance of the Mandarin's head before she answered them.

The case lasted a fortnight and it was several days longer before the Mandarin announced his considered decision.

Ai-weh-deh, the Virtuous One, was appointed official guardian of Ninepence. Her grandparents had left land and money. This would be divided, one half to Ai-weh-deh as legal guardian, one half to the uncle; Ai-weh-deh could have whichever half she desired—the land or the money. That was his decision, and the uncle seemed satisfied by it. Land was useless to Gladys, but the money, which came to almost two hundred dollars, represented a small fortune. It was all used for Ninepence, some of it spent on her education and the rest reserved for her dowry when she married.

CHAPTER EIGHT

THE FRIENDSHIP between the Mandarin of Yangcheng and the little ex-parlormaid from Belgrave Square is probably one of the oddest in the entire history of Eastern and Western relationships. Although Gladys now spoke the local language as fluently as a native, it was years before she managed to dig down through the layers of the Mandarin's mind. He was enigmatic. He regarded her urbanely, his fine, thin face, with its high cheekbones and thin, dark, almond eyes, always impassive. A glossy pigtail dropped from under the round silk cap; the gowns he wore were embroidered in wide scrolls of many colors, invariably beautiful: scarlet, blue, green, gold. To Gladys he always looked as if, by some miracle of time, he had just stepped down from an antique Chinese scroll. His was a feudal society. From his *yamen*, civic authority was administered much as it had been in the time of Confucius. His aides and counselors bore ancient and honorable titles which defined their interest in transport, sanitation, roads, water and so on.

In one of the inner courts was the place of the women. They were not wives, or even concubines, but slave girls, young and lovely creatures purchased with *yamen* funds for the ancient and honorable delights of love. Gladys was not shocked when she understood the implications of the women's court. It was a custom which dated back many hundreds of years; everything was very proper. They were watched over by the older women, most of whom had themselves been *yamen* maidens, and whose daughters would grow up and continue in the same service. They were gay and enchanting girls, singing songs, playing instruments and learning dances—not secluded like harem women of the Middle East, but able to trip through the bazaars fingering the soft silks and buying the combs and cheap jeweled ornaments they adored. Gladys had many friends among them, and often, when she was visiting the Mandarin, she would walk through to the women's court to chat and drink tea with them.

There is little doubt that at first, to the Mandarin of Yangcheng, Gladys Aylward was as alien a species as a creature from the moon. She was female, which meant that in the eyes of man she was socially and intellectually less than dust. Nevertheless, as news of her exploits reached him, and as, over the months, she continually bombarded him with applications, supplications, admonitions and near-threats, he became increasingly aware of her as an individual. Indeed, as their contacts and acquaintanceship increased, the Mandarin of Yangcheng found to his growing astonishment that she was becoming not only an adviser of sorts, but also a friend. By immemorial Chinese standards, he was a highly intelligent man, but his background was circumscribed by the contemplative scholarship of a formal education.

Gladys blew into his *yamen* with a vigor that he had not foreseen. She had had very few years of formal schooling, but she had an intuitive gift for observation and evaluation. She never forgot his first gentle admonition after she had delivered herself of a particularly impassioned piece of Christian propaganda. "Ai-weh-deh," he said softly, "you send your missionaries into our land, which is older by far in civilization than yours. You see us as a nation of heathens and barbarians, do you not?"

"Oh, no! Not by any means," she said.

The Mandarin placed his slender hands in the wide silken sleeves of his robe.

"We have produced great art and great philosophy. The Mandarin speech of China is more beautiful and descriptive than any other in the world. Our poets were singing when Britain was but a rocky outpost on the edge of the known world and America was inhabited solely by redskinned aborigines. Yet you come to teach us a new faith? I find it very strange."

She did not miss the gentle mockery in his voice, and as usual she was willing to argue with him. It was not, however, until many years later that she realized she was witnessing the last years of a Chinese era which had endured for twenty-five centuries.

In the near future, the torrent of communism would flood Old China. The Mandarin and his like would become as extinct as the dodo or the dinosaur. For more than two thousand years the Confucian scholar, not the dialectical commissar, had been the civil servant of China. Caste or birth played but a small part in the scheme of things. They were rulers by virtue of learning, and they controlled the destinies of almost a quarter of the entire human race. The rise to respect and authority of any scholar was the result of years of intense study, and the examination hall was the proving ground of his skill and intellectual superiority.

Of this Gladys was to hear in their long conversations through those ten sunlit years. With a smile and a polite gesture meant to absolve her from any feeling of guilt at belonging to a society as rude and barbaric as that of the West, he told her of his own education. She learned something of the endless toil which had confronted him before he became Mandarin of Yangcheng.

Born of a reasonably well-to-do family in a small town in

North China, for the first seven years of his life he had been allowed to run wild. In the long hot summers, with the other boys, he had scoured the rivers and streams, splashed in the shallows, flown his scarlet kite high against the blue sky, and played the ancient game of catching grasshoppers and locusts and stringing them on slender reeds. He had seen the colored lanterns bobbing in the dark at weddings and funerals, at harvest and threshing times; he had played shuttlecock and gambled with copper *cash*, imitating his elders; and every year he had looked forward to the fourteen-day celebration of the New Year.

When he was six years old, his father had consulted the astrologists to discover a propitious day for the commencement of his school life, and when that day was chosen, the hours of his young summer were over. On school morning, smartly dressed in blue gown, red outside jacket, yellow trousers and navy cap with a scarlet tassel, his head newly shaved, the glossy queue plaited and hanging down his back, he presented himself to his schoolmaster. He opened his first school book. It was a primer on the importance of filial duty, of the nature of man, of the need for education. Because the book was printed with three characters on each line it is known as the *Three Character Classic*; it contains five hundred separate characters, each of which must be learned by heart. From sunrise to sunset, with intervals for meals, he and his schoolfellows worked. Only the writing lessons provided intervals in this prodigious work of memory, and a lesson consisted of copying thousands of different characters onto rice paper with a brush of sable or fox hair, copying and recopying hundreds of times until they were indelibly printed on his mind. A study of the *Three Character Classic*, in the old days, was as far as thousands of Chinese schoolboys ever advanced toward an education. The book was first introduced as a primer of learning a thousand years ago and has been used unchanged ever since. A study of six such books comprises the education of any boy intended for a scholastic career.

Because his parents were moderately well-to-do, the Mandarin decided to continue with his studies. The basis of all his learning was Confucius. "What Confucius teaches is true; what is contrary to his teaching is false; what he does not teach is unnecessary." There were four immense classic volumes of Confucian philosophy to be absorbed.

In all their discussions of Chinese philosophy and ritual, one great question inevitably disturbed Gladys. Why had these carefully regulated codes of behavior which he explained to her, this fine sifting of pure thought by the wisest sages of China, down from generation to generation, not produced a society fit for gods to walk in? Why, at that very moment, were there in every province warring armies, jealous and ambitious men lusting for power. "Why?" she asked him. "Why?"

The Mandarin spread long delicate hands. "The scholar and the soldier exist," he admitted. "One cannot theorize them out of existence. But one hopes that eventually the perfect man will evolve. . . ."

He never tired of explaining the Chinese conception of the "Princely Man."

"The second of the four classic volumes deals with this paragon," he said. "The book is called the *Doctrine of the Mean*. It was compiled by a grandson of Confucius in the year of your calendar some three hundred and thirty-eight years before your Christian prophet was born.

"In this book is depicted the conception of a perfect man, who in all circumstances preserves a golden roundness of character and is thus a model and standard of virtue to all succeeding generations. The perfect man is never satisfied with himself. He that is satisfied is not perfect!"

113

"It seems to me," said Gladys, "that the only concern of Confucius and your other sages was how to pattern life on earth. We in the West believe in life after death. We believe in a Godlike spirit in man which is always present. Are your prophets willing to die for their beliefs?"

The Mandarin of Yangcheng picked up a pale yellow lotus flower from the shallow vase in which it floated, and looked at the waxen texture of the blossom. " 'I love life and I love justice,' " he quoted softly, " 'but if I cannot preserve both I would rather give up life and hold fast to justice. Although I love life, there is that which I love more than life. Although I hate death, there is that which I hate more than death.'

"That was written by Mencius," he said, "a teacher who lived two hundred years later than Confucius. In greatness he is second only to the master himself. 'All men are naturally virtuous,' he wrote. 'Just as water naturally flows downward, the evil of the world contaminates them.' "

In all her conversations with the Mandarin, Gladys never left his presence with a feeling of inferiority or inadequacy. She realized that there was a balance between her practical knowledge and his classical scholarship. Although the teachings of Confucius had permeated down to the humblest peasant in the fields, she possessed a practical faith which was endowed with a spiritual power and a glory beyond the analytical philosophy of Confucius.

In China three religions have met and become embedded in the daily ritual of life: Confucianism, Buddhism and Taoism. A household will worship in the ancestral hall where the tablets to the honorable dead are placed in accordance with the precepts of Confucius; they will also burn incense on the shrine of Buddha; and for a propitious day on which to start a new scholar at school, to hold a marriage, a celebration or a funeral, they will consult a Taoist priest.

Gladys Aylward brought a new religion; she traveled the bare mountains in that wild region, experiencing perhaps the greatest joy a Christian missionary can know, for they were simple peasants she moved among. She met none of the sophisticated resistance, the disillusion and despair of the West: this was a virgin land. She brought a simple faith to uncomplicated people, a faith which answered their needs, a faith which many embraced as devoutly as did those early Anglo-Saxons when the monks of Benedict and Gregory came to their forest clearings, bearing the reassurance that there was, indeed, an infinite Being of goodness, faith and love existing outside the shell of their mortal world.

Yet to her, also, came moments of doubt and indecision. One night, after a long conversation with the Mandarin, they stood together on the balcony at the back of his *yamen* while the sinking sun reddened the whole wild panorama of peaks before them. The peace of that moment had stayed with her even when she reached the courtyard of the Inn of Eight Happinesses and mounted to her room. She paused on the balcony, looked down into the courtyard where the mules bunched darkly together, moved occasionally, snorted and whisked their tails. The moon was rising, its light spilling into the cool fresh mountain sky, brilliant with stars. From the doorway of the downstairs room a fan of yellow light from the castor-oil lamps spread across the level, beaten earth. The gate was shut; the inn was full. She went down into the courtyard, into the muleteers' room, smelly and warm, and there was a hush as the men saw her. They chatted for a few moments, then she sat on the edge of the *k'ang* and began, as she almost always began: "Once upon a time, long ago in a far-off country called Palestine, there lived a man named Jesus Christ. . . ."

She glanced up and saw the light from the flickering oil lamps accentuating and strengthening the features of the men gathered around her. They were simple, kindly peasants, almost as close to nature as the animals with which they journeyed. She knew that their eyes would glisten, their faces quicken with interest as she continued with the story of the faith and strength which had the power to send seven crusades of armored knights across Europe to the Holy Land; which had assuaged the agony of Jeanne d'Arc as her slender body flamed into a human torch, and which had mortised the stones upon which the civilization of the West still stood. She wondered if, in the years to come, any remnant of the faith she preached would stay with them, and be of help to them in their troubles.

She looked at Hsi Lien, the simple muleteer, one of the first of her converts, and one of her friends. He had been in charge of the very first mule team she had hauled into the courtyard; it was he who had fled in terror at the sight of Jeannie Lawson. They had had many a good laugh about that occasion afterward. His home was only a day's journey away, at Chowtsun. But *did* he really understand? Would this faith he had accepted stand him in good stead at a time of trial? Could she just as effectively have told him about Robinson Crusoe and Little Red Riding Hood? Those were also stories. Was the catalyst that turned a legend into a religion only human pain and desperation?

Looking back in the years that followed, she sometimes wondered what she should have done about Hsi Lien. If she could have seen into the future, discerned the terrible tragedy which would befall him, what would she have done? Would she, for his own sake, have sent him out through the city gates, down the mountainside, and away forever from the Inn of Eight Happinesses?

CHAPTER NINE

To GLADYS AYLWARD, those early years in Yangcheng were peaceful and unhurried. There was time to think, time to sleep, time to pray, though it was not always uneventful.

There was the time when the Yellow River flooded, drowning hundreds of people, making thousands homeless, and the refugees trooped back up into the mountains, passing in long streams through Yangcheng and on to Tsechow, Chin Shui and the other cities of the province. There was the time when the great river froze over where it borders the western boundary of Shansi, and Communist troops from Yenan and the province of Shensi walked across the ice. It was a "three coat" winter that year, the coldest in living memory. You judged a winter by the number of quilted coats you had to wear, and a "three coat" winter was cold enough to freeze the tea in the pot. There was heavy fighting around the capital, Taiyuan, far to the north, and the Communist troops infiltrated through the passes as far south as Yangcheng. The posses of resident soldiers under the Mandarin's control elected, at that moment, to chase bandits far from the city; they returned, looking a little sheepish, only when the Communists' three-day occupation was over. The Communists' advance was little more than a reconnaissance in force; they did no damage in the city, although they inflicted much elsewhere. They were not seen again until the Japanese arrived.

There was the time in 1936 when Gladys decided that she

would become a Chinese citizen. She wanted nothing to cut her off from the people, and it was better to be a "Chinese foreigner" than simply a "foreign devil." With the help of the Mandarin she sent off her papers, completed all the formalities and became a naturalized Chinese. It made no difference to her work, or to her relationship with the townsfolk of Yangcheng, but it made her feel as if she belonged to this background.

There was one sadness. Her old friend Mrs. Smith, from the Tsechow mission, on the way to pay her a visit, was taken ill halfway between Tsechow and Yangcheng. The coolies in charge of her mule litter were uncertain whether they should press on to Yangcheng or return to Tsechow; eventually they decided to go on to Yangcheng. The old lady was delirious when she arrived, and died that night without recovering consciousness. Gladys missed old Mrs. Smith, who had been a good friend to her. It was her death that brought new missionaries, the Davises, to Tsechow, one year later, and Gladys made the journey from Yangcheng to welcome them.

She enjoyed immensely these occasional visits to Tsechow. It lay on the plain, and although a walled city also, it was much larger than Yangcheng. One of the great trading centers of south Shansi, it was a terminus for the caravans of small, pouting-lipped, tawny camels which brought down silk and cloth and tobacco from Peking and the northern territories, and took back coal, ironware, chinaware and raw cotton, carried up from the Yellow River and through the Shansi mountains by the mule trains.

It was spring when she arrived, and around the city the apricot and plum trees, the peach and persimmon, were in bloom. From the walls on one side you looked down into the narrow, choked streets of the old city, on the other, out across the patchwork fields of growing crops—corn and mustard seed, cotton, millet, alfalfa and dark green, tall-stemmed sorghum, or *kaoliang*—to the blue-peaked mountains nine miles away.

Jean Davis, the new missionary's wife, a bonnie Scottish lass from Perthshire, never forgot her first sight of Gladys . . . "a wee, thin thing with great, dark, staring eyes," she said, "who rattled away in the Shansi dialect as if she'd been born in the district."

It was true; Gladys had not merely learned the language; she had embedded herself in it. She spoke, thought and dreamed in Shansi dialect; there were no language barriers at all between her and the people with whom she lived.

The arrival of the Davis family, husband, wife and small son, to live at a mission only two days' journey away across the mountains, was a piece of great good fortune for Gladys. They became stanch friends, united in their interests and their work. David and Jean, when they settled down, also dressed and "lived" Chinese. David Davis was a lean, hard young Welshman of thirty-three. Like Gladys, he also visited the loneliest villages to start Christian communities; their parish, through which they both roamed, covered more than five thousand square miles. In many of the isolated villages, the peasants had never seen a white man before, let alone a white woman.

So the years passed. Sometimes Gladys did not see the Davises for months at a time, for it was a long journey from Yangcheng and mainly her work took her out to the lonelier regions. That she left a mark in those places there is little doubt. Even today, if one walked through some of those isolated villages, one would hear the men and women singing Christian hymns as they worked in the fields. She made many converts among them and Christianity altered the lives of those who embraced it.

To the peasants, Christianity was not a foreign doctrine of imperialism; to the women particularly it brought a new life. Under Christianity, they had rights in the household; no longer were they, or their daughters, sold out of hand, or replaced by second and third wives. The idols were burned and a family became a unit, working together. Gladys Aylward was successful in her work because she was different. On one occasion her mother received a letter from a Chinese friend of Gladys's. It ran:

"When your precious daughter came to China, my wife first saw her, and then I talked with her, and found that she is a missionary we need in China. She won't mind the bitternesses, difficulties and poverties, but preaches the Gospel in all the places in the south of Shansi. Most foreigners come to China, not purely for preaching the Gospel, and most of them are very comfortable, and therefore very few people in China believe Jesus Christ. Because the people see that it is not the same what saying in the Bible they have it compared."

Gladys lived her frugal, hard-working life according to "the same what saying in the Bible." She did not know, and no one in Yangcheng realized, that war would soon engulf them as the Japanese, already in power in Manchuria, drove down the age-old routes of the Mongol conquerors. They knew in Yangcheng that there was grave tension in the outside world, that in China the Central Government and the Communists were at war and in almost every province rival warlords conspired and contended for power. Occasionally a detachment of Northern provincial troops would pass through the city, but they quickly moved on and had little contact with the average citizen. In Yangcheng there was a general belief that no one would wish to fight over a small mountain city like theirs. Yangcheng possessed neither the treasure nor the importance enjoyed by a thousand larger, richer and more advantageously located places.

The muleteers, who brought to Yangcheng most of the news and rumor from the world beyond the mountains, understood little of political affairs. Only when the men of southward-bound caravans began to mention that there was concern felt in Luan about a possible Japanese attack, did the people of Yangcheng realize that the Japanese had invaded northern Shansi. And even when reports of battles fought in the north reached them, few citizens in Yangcheng could bring themselves to believe that they would really be affected.

So it was that on that spring morning in 1938, when the little silver planes came droning in over the mountains, everyone ran out of the house to watch them. Many had never seen an airplane before, and these looked very pretty, swooping down out of the sun.

Gladys did not run out of the Inn. At the time, she was kneeling in prayer in an upstairs room with Yang and four converts. She did not hear the aircraft until the last minute, and then the whole world turned into a roaring, falling, confused chaos which ended in blackness. The people in the streets of Yangcheng were still waving and shouting as the black objects fell from the bellies of the aircraft and plummeted down into the town. Their shouts turned to screams of pain and horror as chunks of flying masonry and hissing shrapnel ricocheted among them. The aircraft droned up and down, very low, swooping out over the valley and then back in again. One bomb screamed over the buttress of the city wall and struck a corner of the roof of the Inn of Eight

Happinesses. Nine people in the road outside were killed at once. In the upstairs room where Gladys, Yang, and the others were praying, the floor canted suddenly sideways and they slid and fell downward in a welter of timber, tiles, dust and plaster, to be buried among this debris in the room below.

Gladys remembered hearing faint voices, and then slowly realizing that she was lying face downward with a great weight pressing on her back. She felt no pain, but her breathing was difficult. She could hear voices near by saying, "Praise the Lord, praise the Lord!" Her quick thought was, "This is no time to be praising the Lord. Why don't they do something to get me out?"

Then she heard another voice shouting, "They're there, I know they're there. Under the rubble!"

It seemed hours before Gladys felt the debris being moved. At last they got to her, but a heavy beam pinned her down. When she was finally released, she felt bruised and sick, but she dusted off her clothes and helped to pull out the cook and the others. All of them were suffering from cuts and bruises, but none was seriously injured. The Japanese aircraft had gone, but now there was panic and confusion everywhere.

One man was hopping from foot to foot. "In the town it is dreadful," he was crying. "Everywhere it is blocked; all are killed; it is dreadful, dreadful!"

"We must go and see what we can do, then," said Gladys grimly. "Now, stop that caterwauling and go and lend a hand!" In her bedroom she kept her medicine chest. It contained one large bottle of lysol, one bottle of potassium permanganate crystals, a can of boric acid powder, and absorbent cotton—plenty of absorbent cotton. She rapidly tore her

122

two bed sheets into bandage-sized strips and set off for the East Gate.

Nothing in her life before had prepared her for the sight which confronted her. The walls and gate were untouched, but the center of the town appeared completely pulverized. Dead and dying, wounded and bombshocked, lay everywhere, for the streets had been crowded. The main street was littered with masonry; bodies were half buried beneath it; people still trapped were screaming for help. For a second or two she paused at the gate, quailing momentarily in the face of the task ahead. What could she do with her few silly bandages and the little bottle of permanganate? But the sense of futility passed in a second. To the chattering group of onlookers at the gate she became authoritative.

"I need all of you," she snapped angrily. The surprised townsmen stared at her, then obediently followed her instructions. "Now, get to work. You must all help. You two men clear that rubble over there; someone is buried there. You three, go and get buckets of water—hot water. You—one, two, three, four, five—you'll clear the main street so that there's a free passage. All the dead you'll carry outside the gates. Understand? Now, let's start working at once."

Into the confusion of rubble and masonry and human pain, Ai-weh-deh contrived to bring some modicum of common sense and first aid. A woman lay only a few yards from her, blood streaming from her head. She looked up with agonized eyes. Gladys knelt beside her, put cotton over the wound and tore off a strip of bandage to hold it in place. She saw that the woman was not badly hurt.

"There you are, dear," she said gently. "Now you lie there for a few minutes until you feel better. Do you understand?"

The woman nodded. The terror went out of her eyes. "Yes," she said weakly.

"Where do you live?"

"Outside the walls in the Street of Three Swans."

"Do you think you could walk there if I got someone to help you?"

"I'll try."

Gladys called over one of the men tugging at the rubble. "Listen to me," she said. "In a few minutes this woman will feel strong enough to walk. You'll take her down to her house in the Street of Three Swans. If she cannot walk you will carry her. Make her comfortable in her house, then come back here; there's more work to be done. You understand?"

The man nodded. "Yes, Ai-weh-deh," he said humbly. He helped the woman to her feet, and with her arm around his neck they stumbled off. Gladys moved on.

Two men had uncovered a shopkeeper in the rubble of the first house. They called her over. One look was enough to tell her that he was dead.

"Carry the body outside the walls. Then come back and continue with the work."

In a distance of ten yards or so she dressed the wounds of twelve people. A pail of hot water had appeared and she emptied a few crystals from her precious bottle of permanganate into it. This she dabbed on as a crude antiseptic. When she came across groups of numb, bombshocked survivors, she coaxed or threatened them into action. Her shrill voice echoed through the ruins:

"You three men, get down that hole! Someone's there, can't you hear them calling out? And you others search that building—see no one is in there." Her face streaked with dust and sweat, her tunic stained with blood, she worked steadily on, bandaging and splinting, sponging with permanganate. Once or twice, she sobbed quietly to herself when she happened upon a wounded or dead or mutilated child.

But nothing stopped her working. In the late afternoon, with a sinking heart, she realized that she was still only three quarters of the way up the main street. On the steps of the *yamen* an old man sat, his head in his hands. He was covered with dust but appeared unhurt. As Gladys clambered over the rubble, he raised his head and looked at her with dull eyes.

"So God is still alive," he croaked. "You're still here."

"I'm not God and they can't kill Him," snapped Gladys. "What are you doing, old man, sitting down when there is work to be done?"

"I have been working," he said wearily. "They are all working over there."

Gladys looked in the direction he pointed. At the corner, among the broken masonry, she saw the prison governor.

He was dazed and dirty. "Ai-weh-deh," he said, "I knew that if you were not dead you would be somewhere in the middle of it." He drew the sleeve of his jacket across his brow, leaving a dirty mark.

"You've got people helping?" Gladys asked.

"All the prisoners," said the governor. "They are doing very well."

Even as he spoke Feng, the Buddhist priest, appeared around the corner carrying a wounded man on his back. He smiled at Gladys as he carried his burden past her.

"We're putting the wounded into the *yamen*," explained the governor, dispiritedly. "But there are so many of them. How much longer can we go on like this?"

"Until the job's finished," declared Gladys impatiently. "But we must put some organization into our relief work. We must get the wounded to shelter, the dead buried, and the city cleaned up. Where is the Mandarin?"

"He's in the *yamen*, helping there."

"Let's go and talk to him."

They picked their way over the debris, and found the Mandarin, still in a scarlet gown, talking to a group of shocked officials. At sight of Gladys he dismissed the others and together they tried to decide on a plan. Half an hour later the "relief committee" was functioning. It consisted of the Mandarin, the prison governor, Gladys and Lu Tchen, a shrewd little merchant. Caked with dust and sweat and blood, they sat around a table to formulate plans for the relief of their city. They had no experience; no disaster in their history could be compared with this. Centuries ago the men of Yangcheng had built their walls wisely and well. They had smoothed the outer faces with great square stones, locked and dovetailed into place, and built a second wall behind the first. They had filled the space between with a solid core of granite, making it so wide and strong that a horse and cart could be driven along its top. If cannon were hauled over the mountains, the walls were thick enough to resist a cannonade. Against arrows, spears and catapulted boulders, they were quite impregnable. But against death which plummeted from the heavens, the walls were worse than useless. They had made a tight basket into which the Japanese had aimed their bombs with neat precision, knowing that within those narrow confines the blast effect would create the maximum havoc.

"We must use the muleteers," said Gladys. "We must stop them at the city gates, and tell them they must stable their beasts where they can outside the walls, then work with us to clear the rubble. People are still alive under the ruins. We must get them out and clear the main road."

"There are hundreds of homeless and many wounded," said the governor.

"The temples of Lang Quai and of the Buddhists, in the

center of the city, are unharmed," said the Mandarin. "In one the homeless can live; in the other we can put the wounded."

"We must pool the food supplies, start a communal kitchen, and get cooks to prepare food," said Gladys.

"The merchants will give food and cloth to the hungry and homeless," Lu Tchen suggested.

"Women must be enlisted as nurses," said Gladys, "although I'm afraid many of the wounded will die. The Town Crier must go around and make these announcements. Also, he should instruct people with relatives in the country to go out and stay with them."

"I will see that the muleteers and my prisoners clear the main street from the East to the West Gate," said the governor. "Otherwise all mule trains will be blocked on both sides of the town."

The Mandarin nodded. "I have more disturbing news," he said. "Reports have reached me that the Japanese have captured Luan and are advancing on Tsechow. From Tsechow they will almost certainly march toward Yangcheng. I understand that they are not a merciful people."

"We have several days before they can get here," said Gladys quickly. "We ought not to waste any more time."

The clean-up squads were organized. Muleteers, prisoners and townspeople picked up the chunks of masonry from the main street and tossed them back onto the ruins of its shops and houses. The wounded were carried to the Buddhist temple, where Gladys Aylward, with many helpers, treated them with permanganate. They roughly splinted the broken limbs, tore up sheets to make bandages, comforted the dying as best they could, and sent runners off to fetch relatives of the wounded who could be moved. In a huge pit dug outside the West Gate, close to an ancient cemetery, the dead were

The Small Woman

buried. Yang superintended a squad of cooks from neighboring inns so that no one went hungry. That night hundreds of flickering lanterns burned within the walls of Yangcheng as the work progressed. There was abroad a spirit of comradeship in adversity which in later years so many other citizens of bombed cities all around the world were to experience.

Dawn came in a great flush of crimson. The air was cool and clean; outside the walls the cocks crowed and the dogs barked as they did every morning during the first hour. Inside the walls, only pariah dogs nosed at the rubble in search of food, and no children laughed. The smoke which rose slowly into the clear sky came from smoldering buildings. It was still smoldering five days later when the victorious troops of Japan, in their light khaki uniforms, and carrying efficient-looking packs, came up over the mountain path from Tsechow and entered a deserted city through the East Gate.

CHAPTER TEN

THE JAPANESE entered an empty city, for reports of their ruthlessness had preceded them. Even in Yangcheng the news of their bombings and brutalities was now well known. Out toward the lonely villages and the mountain caves the people streamed, taking what possessions they could. The governor of the prison and his guards assembled the convicts in chains and marched them off to an isolated mountain village. The Mandarin, his wives and family moved to another tiny hamlet nearby. Gladys, with her small Christian community of about forty people, left for Bei Chai Chuang, a tiny walled village of eight houses which lay several miles away to the south, behind the mountain flanking the main mule trail.

Bei Chai Chuang lay on the side of a high peak, like a swallow's nest on a sloping roof. No road led to it, and the rocky terrain over which one passed to reach it left no track across the mountains. In the hollows and clefts protected from the wind, the villagers grew millet and corn, cotton and linseed; they tended their chickens and pigs, sheep and cows, and in season trapped the mountain partridge and pheasant. It was a frugal, simple mode of existence. No Japanese ever discovered Bei Chai Chuang and lived to reveal its whereabouts, and no Japanese ever moved far from his main force in these mountains, for every farmer was a guerrilla fighter, and showed small mercy to those he considered despoilers of his country.

Gladys had many old friends in the village. She had always been welcome there, and now the farmers, even with the many mouths to feed in her group, were hospitable and listened with horror to their stories of the bombing. They stayed at Bei Chai Chuang for over a week, and then news reached them that the Japanese Army had passed through the city and disappeared down the trail.

Gladys decided to go back to recover some property. She had left the deeds to the house and various official passes and papers buried in a box in the courtyard. Bei Chai Chuang seemed a safer place for them than Yangcheng.

It took her several hours to reach Yangcheng, and she approached it cautiously. As she came closer she could see that the West Gate was shut. She skirted the wall, clambering around the narrow apron of rock which dropped steeply to the valley on the *yamen* side of the city, until she reached the East Gate. The houses outside the city were completely deserted; an air of eerie stillness hung over the entire town. The late afternoon shadows were long as she walked down the narrow alleyway to the Inn of Eight Happinesses. The inn sign still creaked in the wind, and it needed a new coat of paint. She went from room to room. It was as they had left it; the corner of the bombed building gaped to the sky. She took a stick and began to grub in the earth in one corner of the courtyard to find the box. She had almost uncovered it when she sensed, rather than heard, movement at the entrance to the courtyard. She turned in alarm. In the doorway, in his dirty tunic and trousers and round black hat, stood the water carrier. She knew him quite well. He was an old man with a goatee, and a thin, sly face. She knew he was a thief and she considered him a wicked old man. She wondered if he had stayed there during the short Japanese occupation. She thought it quite possible; it would provide him with an ideal opportunity to loot.

"When are you leaving?" he asked in his hoarse voice.

She frowned. "Why should I leave? This is my home. I shall sleep here or with one of my neighbors."

"There are no neighbors. Everyone who has come back is in the town, and the gates are locked and barred. You won't get in."

"What does that matter? I can sleep here."

She was annoyed by his attitude. What business was it of his where she went and what she did? She scraped away the last of the dirt and lifted her deed box out of the hole. She opened the lid and examined the contents, wondering if the flimsy papers were really worth preserving. With a war starting, nothing was going to be of much value.

"The Japanese are coming back," said the water carrier, chuckling. Gladys stared at him for a moment without speaking.

"Are you trying to frighten me?" she said coldly. "Because you won't."

"They are already at the West Gate," he said with a snigger.

"Why haven't you gone, then?" retorted Gladys.

"They won't hurt me. They won't bother with a poor old man. But they're at the West Gate, I tell you!"

"Rubbish!" began Gladys, and at that precise moment a reverberating explosion came from the other end of the town. It was so sudden and so startling that she dropped her box and ran. She scurried through the courtyard entrance, and as she ran a succession of other explosions followed. She sped up the alleyway to the East Gate. It was locked and barred. There was no use going along the track eastward; that led to Tsechow, which must be in enemy hands. Bei

Chai Chuang lay to the southwest. She had to skirt the wall again and go in that direction. She wasted no more time, but clawed her way over the boulders in the shadow of the wall. The firing continued. It was almost dusk, and as she rounded the last buttress, she came to an abrupt halt.

A battle was in progress at the West Gate. Beneath it, about fifty Japanese soldiers in light khaki uniforms were sprawled behind rocks, or out in the open, shooting up at the walls above the gate. On top of the wall she could see Chinese Nationalist soldiers firing back and occasionally tossing down a hand grenade which exploded with a sharp crack. Gladys felt a small icy hand reach up from her stomach and grip her heart. The small cemetery in which they had so recently interred the bombed dead lay between her and the battle. She crept quickly into the shelter of its mounds and tombstones. She crouched there, thinking that of all the hiding places she might have chosen a graveyard was the most inauspicious. "But I'm not dead yet!" she told herself. Somehow, she had to get past that battle and reach the mule trail to the west. If she waited until dark she would not be able to see, and she guessed that the main Japanese forces were not far behind this patrol. They might even choose this very graveyard to camp in for the night. That was a grim thought. There was more chance of slipping through this advance guard than of escaping from the main body. These troops were so busy engaging the Chinese that they were paying no attention to their rear. Perhaps if she crept around behind them they might not see her. She would have to go very near, though, for a high mountain wall barred her way on the other side.

Across the trail was a small field of green wheat almost two feet tall, and she hoped that if she could reach its shelter she would be safe. She stood up, and walked quickly forward, skirting behind the ranks of Japanese soldiers, ready to run for it if necessary. Nearing her objective, she broke into a mad run and threw herself headlong into the wheat field. She crawled rapidly away, heedless of the stones and gravel bruising her hands. Finally she reached the steep slope of the mountainside. Across it, hidden from view, she scrambled until she reached the main track leading westward. It led downward into a narrow, steepsided gorge, a mile from the city, which cut for some distance through the mountains. Both sides were sheer. In bad weather a river rushed along the rocky bed, but in fine weather—as it was now—the stream bed was used as a road, supplementing the high, rocky path cut out of the cliffside.

"Suppose," she thought with sudden panic, "I meet another Japanese party in the gorge. I shall be trapped. Which route will they use? The river bed or the high path?"

As she stood there, the panic ebbed, and she was conscious only of her need of aid. "You'll have to help me, Lord," she said aloud. She closed her eyes and began to spin in a small circle, saying: "Whichever path I face when I stop, I shall take. Do You hear me, Lord? Whichever path I face when I stop turning, I shall go along." She spun until she felt dizzy and stopped. She faced directly toward the high path hewn into the side of the gorge overhead. She scrambled up and hurried along it. By now the long shadows of the setting sun filled the canyon, making it a chill and eerie place.

She had gone perhaps half a mile, almost to the place where the gorge swung sharply to the left, when she heard unmistakable noises from ahead and below. It was the sound of an army on the march—of wheels and feet and hoofs clattering over stones. She threw herself flat on her stomach and peered over the edge of the canyon, and she saw that a battalion of Japanese were passing below. They came slowly up

133

the riverbed, a long column of soldiers. They passed fifty feet below her, and she counted heads. There were about five hundred in the battalion, with pack mules and mule-drawn light artillery. She guessed that the guns would soon be trained on the gates of Yangcheng. The soldiers picked their way through the gorge, and Gladys let them rumble out of sight before she risked getting to her feet to run on.

Breathlessly, she reached the place where the high track came down to join the riverbed, scrambled across it and picked her way up the mountainside. When she reached the ridge her heart was pumping heavily. It was almost dark; stars shone high above the peaks. Exhilarated at her escape, she headed along the ridge in the direction of Bei Chai Chuang. She knew she would never reach that village in the darkness, but she accepted calmly the fact that she would have to sleep on the mountainside.

Next morning in the village she told them what had oc-curred at Yangcheng. Many were worried over relatives who might have been unwise enough to return to the city. But they could do nothing. The Bei Chai Chuang men made daily reconnaissances toward Yangcheng, and on the fifth day returned with good news. The gates were open, the Town Crier was parading along the tracks outside the city, banging his gong and shouting, "Will all citizens return and clear their courtyards?"

The refugees from Yangcheng were delighted. Obviously the Japanese had retreated toward Tsechow; now they could return to their homes. Gladys was less confident, not liking the sound of the order, "Clear your courtyards!" She had never, in all her years in Yangcheng, heard that particular proclamation. On the other hand, they had never before been invaded by the Japanese.

She insisted that all her band remain in the village until

she had investigated. With one of the Bei Chai Chuang men, she made the journey over the mountains again. From the heights she looked down at the walls of the city and was suddenly afraid. As they clambered down the rocks toward the mule trail, she became more and more certain that horror lay inside those old walls. The absence of movement, of noise, of rising smoke, the lack of signs of life, all contributed to a frightening sense of physical oppression.

The West Gate was open and they walked slowly under the arch, every step confirming her fears. It was a city of the dead. A city of hollow-eyed corpses piled along the main street and in every alleyway. Most had been bayoneted, a few shot. All along the streets, in the temples, in the bazaars, the bodies crouched or lay, twisted grotesquely. There were women and children, too. In the angular, disinterested rigidity of death, the bodies clogged the city, and the dogs, the horrible pariah dogs, were surfeited with flesh. The air smelled of death. With a set face Gladys walked along the main street. She shed no tears. No tears would come. These bodies were past pity or tears; one could not weep for corpses in a charnel house. Her emotions were frozen into a tight kernel of horror.

A small crowd huddled outside the *yamen*. She pushed her way through, and in the inner chamber discovered the Mandarin. His face was gray. She came straight to the point.

"They must be buried," she said flatly.

He nodded, passing a thin hand across his brow. Like Gladys, he had arrived at Yangcheng from his mountain hide-out only that morning. He had seen and heard what had occurred. With no sign of the Japanese in the city, many of the townsfolk had come back into Yangcheng to pick up their lives again. It was then that Chinese guerrilla troops had retreated into the city, attacked by the Japanese advance

135

guard. As the Mandarin explained the sequence of tragedy, Gladys nodded. She had seen the opening skirmishes of that action. Infuriated at resistance, at being denied access, the Japanese had surrounded the city until their main army arrived, then beaten in the gates. With systematic fury they had butchered every man, woman and child they found within. Not even Jenghiz Khan could have slaughtered so ruthlessly, and Yangcheng in past centuries had experienced the wrath of his warriors.

A huge pit was dug outside the West Gate at the edge of the cemetery which already contained the victims of the bombings. The dead were heaped into it. In the courtyard of the Inn of Eight Happinesses, Gladys found three more bodies sprawled. She helped to bury them on the mountainside some distance away. She stayed until late afternoon in the city, but suddenly overwhelmed by the tragedy, which grew into a great sickness in her mind, she could stand it no longer. Abruptly she decided not to spend the night in Yangcheng, but to return at once to Bei Chai Chuang. She walked back through the town, past the grisly procession of citizens carrying their dead to the pit, and out under the West Gate, and her sorrow was scarcely bearable.

From the mountain above she looked back at the town which had been such a well-loved home for so many years. With the sun low, the roofless pagodas were black silhouettes against the sky; the ruin was masked in shadow. The walls still sloped up, strong and elegant as ever. It looked like a city intact, a remote mountain city of peace and beauty built by ancient, skilled hands. But everything had changed; what she saw was only a shell, a husk; in two short weeks the city she loved had perished.

She might return and live in that city; perhaps she would rebuild the roof of the Inn; but it would never be the same again. No cleansing, or rebuilding, could ever remove the memory of its death, or erase these recent horrors from her mind. The time of peace was over. This remote and wind-swept territory she had come to know and adore was now a battlefield. With a deep sigh, she turned away and went on slowly over the mountains toward the village of Bei Chai Chuang.

As usual, she was up just after dawn. Ten days had passed since the sacking of Yangcheng. She walked around the balcony and down the stone steps into the courtyard, leaving the room she shared with ten other women and the children. In the kitchen she gulped down the steaming bowl of millet with her chopsticks, swallowed scaldingly hot twig tea from a small china bowl. Outside the house it was cool, for the sun was still not above the peaks, and there was a fragrance and a sharpness in the air. She stood for a moment breathing deeply, looking down into the valley, and across at the distant heights. Then she hurried over to her improvised hospital to start the day's work. As she walked into the cave, the ten patients lifted their heads and greeted her.

She was brisk and cheerful, as much like all those intimidating nurses she remembered from her childhood as she could manage. "Good morning," she said. "Have you slept well? Time to give you all your medicine."

The hospital cave lay within the village wall. The wall itself was built so closely into the contour of the mountain-side that from a distance you could not distinguish it from the natural stone. The mountain towered above it like a cliff, and below the village the ground fell away sharply.

In the side of the mountain, within the wall, in the center of the village, was the cave. The men of Bei Chai Chuang had used it as a stable for their animals; when the heavy winter snows came they packed all their livestock into its shelter. With their help Gladys had cleaned it out and made it her hospital. The sacking of Yangcheng had made this a humanitarian necessity. Many wounded had dragged themselves or been carried to refuge in this village. In the next few weeks there were going to be many more casualties needing attention. Japanese aircraft on patrol machine-gunned and bombed whenever the inclination seized them, and enemy patrols fired at any villager they saw working in the fields or on the mountainside. Francis, one of Gladys's children, caught in the open by an attacking plane, received a bullet through his hand and lost three of his fingers.

News soon spread of Ai-weh-deh's improvised hospital at Bei Chai Chuang, and the sick and wounded crawled toward it. Most of the injured suffered from gunshot wounds. These she treated as best she could. She had castor oil, sulphur, the inevitable potassium permanganate, and a big metal syringe given to her in Tsechow. In the cave, Chung Ru-mai, the Bible Woman, a visitor from Tsechow trapped by the sudden Japanese advance, boiled the water and dissolved the crystals. Gladys carefully filled her syringe and turned to the first patient. He was a young farmer from the fields near Yangcheng. A bullet had passed through the calf of his leg. He smiled as she approached and pulled up the blue cotton trouser leg.

"Hold the bowl underneath," directed Gladys.

Syringing the wounds with permanganate was her stand-by treatment. It proved an effective remedy, for only one of her patients died. He was also a young farmer. A Japanese bullet had smashed his elbow and glanced off into his stomach. Not all her patience and care and syringing could save him.

That spring offensive of the Japanese down the ancient

Shansi mule trails toward the Yellow River was obviously
only a preliminary foray. In the early autumn their forces
evacuated Tsechow and pulled back as far as Luan. Their
limited offensives in North China during those early months
of the war were experimental probes into difficult terrain.
In the spring and early summer they moved into the mountains, following the old trade routes, overcoming any pockets
of resistance with the ruthlessness and barbarity which had
characterized every enemy from the north since the days of
the earliest Mongol invasions. After passing through Yangcheng they pressed on as far as Chowtsun. Here they captured many people, including Hsi Lien, the muleteer whom
Gladys knew so well. A rapid advance patrol had surprised
him at home with his family, his wife and three children.
Grinning, the stocky Japanese soldiers had prodded him outside. "Here is a good strong muleteer," they said. "You will
serve as an ammunition carrier and no harm will come to
you and your family. You understand?"

"But I cannot," faltered Hsi Lien. "I am a Christian. I am
a pacifist. If I carried your bullets, I would be helping in
your war. I cannot do it."

They took him before an officer and Hsi Lien repeated
his beliefs, and affirmed his refusal to aid them.

"In that case," said the Japanese officer pleasantly, "we
will show you how we treat Christians who refuse to co-
operate."

They tied him to a post outside his own home, barricaded
the door so that his wife and three children could not get
out, and then set fire to the house. They jeered at him as the
screams of the trapped woman and children drove Hsi Lien
to the verge of madness. They left him tied there while the
flames still burned, and retreated to Yangcheng to continue
their butchery within the city walls. When night fell Hsi

Lien's neighbors crept down from the hills and released him. Demented, he made for the mountains. He had heard that Gladys was at Bei Chai Chuang.

He burst in upon her, incoherent with grief. It was some hours before they could get the story from him. Gladys listened in silence. There was little she could do to comfort him, but at least they could give the bodies of his family Christian burial. A small party—Gladys, the Bible Woman, two strong farmers, and Hsi Lien—set off over the mountains toward Chowtsun. They came down into the village at dawn, and with a few villagers, gathered in the courtyard heaped high with blackened embers.

Gladys stood on a heap of stones, raised a little above the others. They bowed their heads as she read aloud from her Bible:

Let not your heart be troubled; ye believe in God, believe also in me. In my Father's house are many mansions: if it were not so, I would have told you. I go to prepare a place for you. And if I go and prepare a place for you, I will come again, and receive you unto myself; that where I am, there ye may be also. And whither I go ye know, and the way ye know.

She looked at Hsi Lien, the muleteer, who stood with head bowed, the tears running down his cheeks, a man now without son, daughter, wife or home, and her heart went out to him in helpless pity. When she rode back over the mountains to Bei Chai Chuang, she took him with her.

Through the autumn, winter and the early spring of 1939, Gladys divided her time between Bei Chai Chuang, Yangcheng and the villages in the province where she had established small Christian communities.

Her job as a foot inspector had ended. It was a luxury occupation which did not survive the bombing. There were more important things to do now. The Inn of Eight Happinesses also was failing. The mule traffic along the ancient route had almost stopped, for with Luan in enemy hands travelers could go no farther than Tsechow. On this curtailed route a few of her old muleteer acquaintances still called, but Yang, the cook, had disappeared, and with him had gone much of the spirit of the place. When the Japanese first invaded Yangcheng, he had gone back to his native village in the mountains. He did not return. What happened to him Gladys never discovered, but news reached her that he was dead. She never found out how he died. He was an old man and it could have been from natural causes, but, somehow, she could not quite believe this. He was such a rebellious, impatient old fellow that the idea of his taking to his bed and quietly passing seemed most unlikely. She was deeply distressed by the news of his death; he had been a stanch friend when she most needed friendship.

These days she was always short of money. From time to time her mother sent a money order, and with the rate of exchange so high, a few shillings would last her for months. Not that money mattered very much, for she was a tradition in the region by now, and among the Chinese in those troubled years, when you had food and shelter you shared it with those in need.

In that spring of 1939, the news that the Japanese were moving in through the mountains again sent more panic blowing through the streets of Yangcheng. Reluctant to abandon their homes and their livelihoods, the people had slowly returned, hoping that some miracle might prevent another Japanese advance. They reasoned that the first disaster could have been bad luck; it might never happen again. The orders of the Chinese Nationalist commander in the district destroyed all these illusions. His dictum, supported by the High Command, was harsh.

"A scorched earth policy!" he said. "Burn your crops. Leave your houses roofless. Let there be no shelter for the invaders anywhere!"

In despair, the peasants watched the soldiers burning the stalks of the green millet and corn upon which their very existence depended. "But what shall we do?" they pleaded. "How can we live without grain?"

"Take to the hills," was the reply. "Live in the caves and mountains, and grow your crops in every fold or valley where you find fertile earth. Prey on the invader like locusts! Kill his men! Steal their supplies! Take the rifles from the dead and turn them against the Japanese. Only in this way can we save China."

Gladys looked ruefully at her gaping roof; the bomb and the winter weather had made a scorched earth policy quite unnecessary. The Mandarin was greatly troubled. He called her to see him.

"This policy of destruction is difficult," he said. "We have done almost everything that the soldiers desired, but there is still this Pagoda of the Scorpion."

"What about it?" said Gladys. "It's an ugly old place!"

"As you may know, there is a legend attached to its history. Hundreds of years ago, so it is said, a giant scorpion roamed these mountains destroying many people. While it was sleeping, the people brought great blocks of stone and built the pagoda around and over it, imprisoning it forever. Now the townspeople are afraid that if they destroy the pagoda the scorpion will escape."

"And you really believe that?" Gladys asked.

He smiled, "No, I do not believe it; that is why I wish you

and your Christians would accept the task of pulling it down!"

"With the greatest of pleasure," Gladys said quickly, with the slightly self-righteous satisfaction of a good Christian allowed to destroy a work of idolatry. "I'll get the men in from Bei Chai Chuang, too. We'll start on that horrible heathen temple first thing tomorrow morning."

"When you have finished," said the Mandarin, "I am giving a feast which I would like you to attend. It will probably be the last ever held in the town of Yangcheng, as we are leaving little that is useful. I have something to say I wish you to hear."

Next morning, several dozen Christians attacked the Pagoda of the Scorpion with a variety of implements. It did not take them long to pry the stones apart and raze it to the ground.

When the Mandarin's feast was held, Gladys, to her surprise, found that although as usual she was the only woman present—that had been her privilege for many years—on this occasion she was sitting beside the Mandarin, in the seat of honor at his right hand. This had never happened before. All the important personages of Yangcheng were present: the governor of the prison, two wealthy merchants, several officials—about a dozen in all. The meal was simple, unlike the sumptuous feasts she had enjoyed in early years, and which had lasted for hours.

Toward the close the Mandarin stood up and made his speech. He recalled how Ai-weh-deh had first come to Yangcheng; how she had worked for them; what she had done for the poor and the sick and the imprisoned; of the new faith called Christianity which she had brought with her, and which he had discussed with her many times. Gladys was puzzled by his references. He sounded so much like the chairman of a local committee back in England that she wondered if he were going to present her with an illuminated address or a silver teapot. But after speaking for some minutes he turned very gravely toward her and said seriously: "I would like, Ai-weh-deh, to embrace your faith. I would like to become a Christian!"

Around the table arose a murmur of astonishment. Gladys was so astounded that she could hardly speak. The guests nodded and smiled, and she knew that she was expected to reply. She got up and stuttered her surprise, her appreciation and her thanks. The Mandarin saw her confusion and helped her out. "We will talk of all details later, Ai-weh-deh," he said. She sat down, realizing that she had made her most important convert since coming to China.

The talk then turned to the approach of the Japanese, and how they would evacuate the city. The governor of the prison had his problem. When the enemy first arrived he had marched all his prisoners off into the country and kept them manacled in a cave in the mountainside. Feeding and guarding them had been most difficult; he did not think he could do it again. Should he release the prisoners or execute them? The guests discussed his dilemma. There seemed to be general agreement that execution was the safer plan; there were murderers and desperate men among the convicts. Only Gladys protested. Surely, there must be some better way? Why not release them on security or bail, in the custody of friends or relatives who could be responsible for their behavior? Yes, the Mandarin was in favor of that solution, and the governor nodded agreement. He would try her plan, but if the Japanese came too close and there were convicts still without guarantor, he was afraid he would have to behead all who remained.

On the East and West Gates next day, notices were posted

proclaiming this procedure. They stated that friends and relatives could come and claim a prisoner, if they would guarantee his future behavior, and pay ninety cents as a token of good faith. The Town Crier was sent around the streets to shout the same announcement.

Gladys visited the jail next day. The response had been reasonable, but there were still twelve prisoners left with no friends or relatives to claim them. As she entered the dismal courtyard, Feng, the Buddhist priest, and another man, Sheng Li, with whom she had had many conversations, came forward to greet her. By local standards Sheng Li was an educated man. He could read and write, and was well acquainted with Chinese finance. So well-versed had he been in this particular art that he had forged a *tucheng*, a stone seal used by wealthy men to stamp their official papers. Each bears its own distinctive markings. Sheng Li had forged the *tucheng* of a wealthy merchant, and by using it discreetly had made a pleasant income until his deception was discovered.

He was a jolly little man, and Gladys was very fond of him. He had been sentenced to fifteen years in prison. Now, on impulse, she said she would act as his guarantor. She paid over the ninety cents. But as she prepared to leave the courtyard with the reprieved Sheng Li, she was dramatically aware of the dejected eyes of Feng trying not to look toward her. She sighed in resignation. Of what use was friendship if an extra ninety cents could not be found? "I will be guarantor for Feng also," she said. Her reward was immediate in every line and muscle of the man's face. He said nothing; he did not have to speak; happiness and gratitude radiated from him.

Followed by the two free men, Gladys went back to the Inn of Eight Happinesses and began to make arrangements for their departure for Bei Chai Chuang. This time she intended to be out well before the Japanese arrived.

Next morning she went to take leave of the Mandarin and the governor of the prison. The governor was still most disturbed; he had eight prisoners left, two of them were condemned murderers, and no guarantors had come forward to take them off his hands.

"How did those two commit murder?" asked Gladys.

"In the Green Pagoda," said the governor. "The idols had valuable jewels in their ears and eyes. They were caught by one of the priests in the act of prying them out. They murdered him while trying to escape!"

"Oh!" said Gladys contemplatively. She decided she would not feel particularly happy with those two around.

She went to see the remaining convicts in the prison. Eight dejected pairs of eyes stared up at her. She questioned them all and learned that each one had relatives living in outlying villages but there was no chance whatsoever of the news of the amnesty reaching these villages before the Japanese arrived. She said "Um!" to herself three or four times, and considered the risks, then she turned to the governor.

"I can't pay ninety cents for each of these men; I haven't that much money. But if you agree, they can come with me and I'll be responsible for their behavior. I'll send messengers to their relatives in each village as soon as I reach Bei Chai Chuang. And as I get the securities I'll send them off."

The governor nodded; not only was he in full agreement with any solution to his dilemma, but also firmly convinced by now of the rightness of most of Ai-weh-deh's decisions.

The official in charge of the women's court also came to see her with a problem. One of the young slave girls, Sualan, was troubling him. She was very young and pretty and gay,

146

and almost of marriageable age. As the *yamen* was moving, and the women were dispersing to many villages, he did not know what to do with her. All the officials had their wives and concubines to attend to. There was not time to marry Sualan off. It was not fair that she should be left alone and unchaperoned after living such a sheltered life in the women's court. Who could say what might become of her, men being the creatures they were?

"All right," said Gladys resignedly, "she can come with me and my criminals, and I'll look after her. It'll be quite a new experience for her. For me, too, I expect," she added.

So they set off for Bei Chai Chuang, Gladys and her small band of Christians, and Sualan the pretty slave girl, with the convicted thieves, rogues and murderers trailing not uncheerfully in the rear. The convicts gave her no trouble whatsoever. They remained peaceably at Bei Chai Chuang, while messengers went out to their villages to obtain the pledges of responsibility from their relatives. Eventually only Feng and Sheng Li remained, and they stayed with her for a very long time.

In Bei Chai Chuang, in the early spring, the news reached her that one of her Christian converts in a village beyond the town of Chin Shui had been attacked by bandits. Although he was a poor man, a rumor had reached the bandits that he possessed a hidden hoard of gold, and they swept down from the mountains, broke into his home, and tortured him in an effort to make him reveal the whereabouts of the mythical treasure.

With Timothy, a nine-year-old orphan boy who had also joined the ever-growing troop of children at the Inn, and Wan Yu, a seventeen-year-old girl who lived in a village some miles from Chin Shui and wished to visit her mother, Gladys set off to see if she could help this peasant. They found him in his home, very sick. The bandits had burned him horribly with red hot irons. She dressed his burns and made him as comfortable as she could. It was a quiet village in a hidden valley, and the terraced fields were still green with spring corn. They stayed there for more than a week; it was peaceful and serene and Gladys enjoyed the short holiday. Chin Shui was two and a half days' travel away, Yangcheng was even farther. Each morning she climbed a near-by hill and sat at the top looking at the clouds and the far-stretching mountains, forgetful of the war. But her days of serenity were short-lived. A messenger came running—literally running—from the small Christian Mission she had set up at Chin Shui. The Japanese had entered Yangcheng again and were expected to sweep on into Chin Shui any day now. There were two hundred refugees in the Mission. Could she come and help at once?

She scrambled her few belongings together and set off with Timothy and Wan Yu. They spent the first night at Chersin, a small village, and listened that night to a heavy thunderstorm beating on the tiles. It delayed their departure next morning, as the road was impassable with slippery mud. As soon as the hot sun began to dry it out, they set off again. Chersin was only two miles behind them when they heard the noise of an airplane and saw it beginning to circle above their heads. They ran for shelter. Flat on the ground, they heard the bombs whistle down in the distance and explode, and with mixed feelings, Gladys realized that it was Chin Shui, their destination, still a day's journey ahead of them, that was under attack.

They arrived next morning in time to witness the now almost familiar pattern being repeated. All the citizens were assembled in the courtyard of a large temple in the center of the city, and here the Mandarin of Chin Shui made his announcement. The city had been bombed, therefore they could expect the enemy to follow up the bombing. Everyone must leave the town not later than first light the next day.

As she listened to the voice of this tall thin figure in his Mandarin's robes, standing on the gray stone steps of the temple with pagoda roofs and the city wall framed behind him, and the hot blue sky and the mountains beyond, Gladys realized how often through the centuries such a scene must have been enacted. The invaders invariably came from the north, bringing blood and death and destruction. The people fled to the mountains, then crept back again when the enemy had gone, to bury their dead and rebuild their homes. It had happened to generation after generation. If not a foreign invader, then it was some upstart warlord. In ten years' time, who would remember on which day the Japanese had attacked, and who had been killed, and what damage had been done? Yes, the mother who lost her son, and the widow mourning her husband, they would remember. But soon they, too, would grow old and forget, and the eternal pattern of birth and death, sowing and harvesting, would be re-established. It was then she realized that God had fashioned them well, these mountain people. For her part she would never abandon them, no matter what happened.

In a letter sent home that year to her mother, on a grubby scrap of paper, she wrote: "Do not wish me out of this or in any way seek to get me out, for I will not be got out while this trial is on. These are my people; God has given them to me; and I will live or die with them for Him and His Glory."

149

CHAPTER ELEVEN

THAT NIGHT, in the courtyard of the small Mission house at Chin Shui, Gladys made her decision. They, too, must leave if the enemy were advancing. Yangcheng was already overrun; they could not go back there. Therefore she must try to get back with Timothy and Wan Yu to Bei Chai Chuang, where her friends and the rest of the children were waiting. These days there was safety only with people you knew and could trust. Chinese bandits were joining with larger formations, recruiting from the homeless villagers, becoming, in effect, guerrilla forces. All were lawless and savage, and when the inclination took them, they could be crueler to their own people than the Japanese. Gladys knew that, if she took to the mountains, she could, at least, avoid the advancing Japanese. Against other enemies they would have to take their chance.

At first light next morning Gladys, Wan Yu and Timothy left the Mission and walked out through the East Gate carrying their bundles. Darkness still clung to the valleys; but the sky was lightening rapidly above the peaks ahead, and the cocks were brazenly warning the city that both day and the Japanese were advancing.

They had walked no more than three hundred yards when she felt the stirrings of a strange uneasiness. They had two miles to cover before they could reach the rocky shelter of the mountains, and some instinctive sense made her apprehensive. There was no visual reason for the oppression of fear she suddenly experienced, but she believed in her intuitions. Suppose the Japanese had patrols operating on each side of their advancing troops? Suppose they were trapped in a gorge by these patrols? It had almost happened to her outside Yangcheng. She frowned at Timothy and Wan Yu.

"We're going back," she announced loudly. They looked at her in astonishment. "But why?" said Wan Yu.

"I don't know. But we are!" She grabbed Timothy's hand, turned on her heel and marched briskly back toward the city gates, tugging him along behind her.

"We can go and stay at my village," said Wan Yu eagerly, hurrying after her. "It lies in a valley out through the West Gate. My brother will look after us. He is a very nice man."

"All right, we'll go and stay there," said Gladys. "I just have an idea it's too dangerous to try to get to Bei Chai Chuang just now."

They hurried back through the East Gate. The streets were boiling with people. Men, women and children, laden with household goods, streamed through the streets, making for the West Gate. As they hurried along with the crowd Gladys heard a voice behind her calling: "Ai-weh-deh! Ai-weh-deh!" She looked around. It was the postmaster, a small, eager, fussy individual whom she knew only slightly. He carried a bulky brown paper parcel tied together with string.

"There are letters for you," he gabbled, thrusting the parcel at her. "They were sent on from Yangcheng. All the postoffice documents and stamps are in it, too. Will you look after it for me?"

"But why can't you look after it yourself?" she demanded in an aggrieved voice. "Why tie my letters up with all your stuff?"

"It is necessary. You are the safest one."

"But it's not my job," she began, and stopped in mid-sentence. From the gate by which they had just re-entered came the noise of a fusillade of shots and screams of terror. The Japanese advance troops had arrived. If her intuition had not been correct, they would have walked right into them. There was immediate panic; whereas everyone had been walking, now they were running. Larger baskets and bundles were jettisoned in a wild scramble for the West Gate. Men, women and children poured from houses and alleyways and joined the confusion.

The postmaster dropped the parcel at Gladys's feet and ran for his life. Instinctively she stooped to pick it up. It was heavy, too big to carry under her arm; she struggled along carrying it in both arms on top of her bedding, determined not to abandon the precious letters from home. Timothy and Wan Yu scurried along beside her, carrying bundles of Bibles from the Mission, also too precious to abandon.

Outside the West Gate the road ran parallel to the swift-flowing Chin River. There was a ford three hundred yards from the gate. Wan Yu's village lay across the river and far up in a steep valley on the other side. Most of the towns-people were making for the ford. Amid a swarm of them, Gladys, Wan Yu and Timothy waded the river. It was chest-deep to Gladys; she jettisoned her bedding and balancing the postoffice parcel on her head with one hand, clutched Timothy with the other. In midstream she thought suddenly how ridiculous she must look, fleeing from the Japanese with a brown paper parcel containing all the paraphernalia of the Chin Shui postoffice balanced on her head. But she did not stop. Safely across the river, their garments clinging clammily to their legs and bodies, they began to scramble up the mountainside, spurred on by the sound of rifle fire cracking through the city streets behind them.

There were no paths. They panted up through terraced fields to the broad valley, flanked by steep peaks, and continued up through millet patches. All that day they climbed, barely pausing to rest. The noise and confusion died away behind them. The valley stretched upward for many miles, hemmed in closely by mountains. Wan Yu's village lay almost at the top of the valley, with only one other above it. At any other time the location would have been idyllic, for from the village the valley sloped downward to the Chin River, a winding, sun-glossy streak far below. Where the valley joined the deep cleft of the river bed, on the flat ground, stood the walled city they had just left, now in the hands of the Japanese.

It was high summer and, in the sheltered valley terraces, roses bloomed, bees clung to the blossoms, pigs and chickens nosed and scratched in the hard-baked earth, and, swooping overhead, eagles looked down with sharp eyes at the unfamiliar smoke rising from the villages along the river banks and the lower slopes of the valley.

In Wan Yu's house lived her old mother, her brother and his wife. Within a few hours of their arrival they were joined by many others fleeing from the Japanese. To these poor creatures the house of Wan Yu's brother became a final haven. They could go no farther. Among them were two old blind men, several grandfathers, four pregnant women, several others with small babies and half a dozen other children. It was quite impossible to think of traveling farther across the mountains with such a party. Several were injured. Once again Gladys turned the house into an improvised nursing home and dressing station, and prayed that the Japanese would come no closer.

Practically every day the enemy troops came out of their Chin Shui headquarters and systematically ravaged the seven villages which lay at intervals along the river bank. But they were back inside the walls, with the gates locked, by nightfall. Almost every night, holding aloft their lanterns, Gladys and the farmers went down into the valley to aid dazed or wounded peasants. She knew it was only a matter of time before the enemy turned their attention to the villages lying farther up the valley, but as Wan Yu's house was so far away, she hoped they would never reach them. Refugees were constantly moving through their village and on into the mountains beyond. As a small measure of safety, Gladys arranged a system of watchers to man a spy hole knocked in the courtyard wall, during the daylight hours.

Five weeks after they had entered Chin Shui, the Japanese started to raid the villages lying farther up the valley, and now they were pressing farther and farther afield. As the raids came closer, Gladys realized that, even though the house was packed with old and sick, they could expect no mercy from the Japanese. Chinese guerrilla bands were constantly attacking the enemy on these forays, and the Japanese treated each village as a possible hiding place.

The news that the small woman who possessed a God with magical powers of protection lived in the village had reached many people, and a constant stream of supplicants was the result. On the afternoon that the Japanese came, she was tending one of the sick women in an upstairs room. Even before her door banged open she heard Wan Yu's shrill scream: "They're here, they're here!"

Quickly she ran downstairs and across to the hole in the courtyard wall. She peered out. Theirs was the first house in the village; only a small temple about fifty yards away lay farther down the valley. She could hear the priests blowing horns, banging drums and offering up obeisances which were supposed to drive the Japanese away. As she watched, she saw a number of khaki-clad figures advance through the terraces and group near the temple. They talked among themselves. Some of them went toward the temple; others started toward Wan Yu's house. Inevitably the next place they entered would be this courtyard, unless she did something to prevent it. "Hide yourselves, quickly," she shouted to Wan Yu. "I'll try to keep them out."

She ran to the front gate. She did not know what to do. She only knew she must stop them, even to the extent of going out and fighting them with her bare hands. If she appeared by herself, perhaps the sight of a "foreign devil" in such an unusual place might occupy their attention for a time. Perhaps they would even forget the others. The outside door was solid, the latch of heavy iron, and as she got to it her courage ebbed away. She leaned against the door, turning so that her back was braced against it for support. Her clenched hand went to her heart to try to stop its pounding. For perhaps ten seconds she stood there, reaching with desperate mental agony for strength. Then into the confusion of her mind, with the clarity of an articulate voice, burst the phrase: *My grace is sufficient for thee: because my strength is made perfect in weakness.* She stood straight, and the feeling of panic seeped away. Then she turned, pressed down the latch, swung open the heavy door and stepped out into the bright sunshine, abruptly aware of Wan Yu's piping voice from the balcony behind her.

"Ai-weh-deh, they've turned back! They're going down the valley! They're going away!"

She felt the sunshine warm on her face. She tried to call back to Wan Yu, but found her mouth too dry. Her legs felt weak; she sat down quickly on the step of the doorway and breathed slowly and deeply. When she went inside the old women were crying in relief.

The Japanese never returned to Wan Yu's village. The weeks passed and in the late summer they pulled back from Chin Shui, back along the trail to Yangcheng and then through to Tsechow, where they spent the winter. When the news of their retirement reached Gladys, she went back to Chin Shui with Wan Yu and Timothy. She carried with her the brown paper parcel containing the postoffice equipment, and handed it over to the rather shamefaced official. She went out along the mule trail, over the mountains to Bei Chai Chuang, and then on again to Yangcheng and the Inn of Eight Happinesses.

She looked at it sadly. The roof still gaped where the bomb had struck; the Japanese had stabled their horses in what had once been the Mission hall. It was filthy, but she made it as habitable as possible. The people came in from the caves and mountain villages and repaired their houses, and a thin flicker of life seemed to rekindle in the old city. The Mandarin came back with his entourage and set up again in his *yamen*. The governor of the prison returned with his soldiers. A few mule trains drifted up from the south and a few shopkeepers reopened with a dwindling supply of commodities. But only when the heavy snows sealed the passes did anyone really feel safe in his bed.

In February, with the snow beginning to clear, Gladys decided she would visit the Davises in Tsechow, even though it was occupied by the Japanese. She had had no word from them for many months and was worried. From reports which filtered through from Tsechow she had heard that the Japanese were not ill-treating the inhabitants. The Mission and compound at Tsechow lay outside the walls of the city, and although the Japanese maintained a fairly strict surveillance on those passing through the gates, they could not, and did not, keep a check on the hundreds of peasants and refugees who were constantly milling around the city.

Gladys believed that she could pass as a humble Chinese peasant, and as she arrived at night when even the boldest Japanese was locked within the city walls, it was a comparatively easy journey. She was welcomed warmly by Jean and David.

They told her they had not been badly treated. This was the second time they had lived under Japanese occupation, and so far they had not been molested. Periodically the Japanese searched the Mission, but they had not behaved too objectionably. During the first occupation, apparently the enemy and the townspeople had got on quite well, David Davis told her. Individually, he had found that many of the officers were pleasant people, and to his surprise some of them, if not actually Christians, were interested in discussing Christianity. Sometimes Japanese soldiers would attend his Christian services. Nevertheless, although ostensibly Japan and Britain were still friendly nations, he could feel the antagonism.

He warned Gladys to be careful, very careful. He was glad of her appearance at this time, however, because he hoped she would help to run the Mission while he escorted two elderly European ladies who were still in Tsechow out of the danger area and away to Chefoo on the coast, a month's journey away. More and more now this area of Shansi was becoming a battlefield. There were thousands of guerrillas in the mountains. The troops of the local warlord had been joined by Chiang Kai-shek's Nationalist forces; the whole territory bristled with resistance points. Gladys had observed how poorly equipped were the Northern troops in those early days. They did not lack courage, but there was never more than one rifle for every four or five men. In battle, they would wait until the rifleman died so that another could seize the weapon and continue the fight. When Chiang Kai-shek's troops arrived, better equipped and supported by the sturdy Northerners, they soon showed the Japanese that their life as military conquerors was going to be an uncertain one indeed. Intermittently entering into the conflict, also, were Communist troops from Szechwan, as busy attacking the Chinese Nationalists as the Japanese. It was a war of desperate attrition by all concerned, in which no quarter was asked or given.

In the mission at Tsechow, where David Davis tried to retain some aspect of neutrality, there were well over a hundred orphans and refugee children, as well as many adult refugees. Gladys quickly lost her awe of the Japanese, and was soon asking their supply sergeants for food—and receiving it. They were a constant puzzle; she could never reconcile their intermittent courtliness and kindness with their many acts of ferocity. Most of the Japanese soldiers were fond of children; and one day a party of them entered the compound with sacks of sugar, which they emptied into three large water jars. Then, with shouts of laughter, they began to serve every child with the sweetened mixture. Whenever their troops returned to Tsechow after a military victory, they were given a three-day holiday, and the city gates were locked while they indulged in their violent orgies.

The mission at Tsechow was large and rambling; the men's and women's courts were far apart. David Davis lived with his wife and family near the men's court, Gladys quite close to the women's court. It was she, therefore, who first heard the screams and shouts one night when a party of Japanese soldiers and officers, who had crept in through the front gate, began to smash down the doors of the women's rooms around their courtyard. There were at least a hundred women staying there, refugees, converts, visitors from out-side villages.

As she ran into the courtyard, a Japanese officer saw her and snapped a command to a private carrying a rifle. With-out warning, he swung the gun and crashed the butt against her head. She fell, barely conscious, realizing only that the rifle butt was still clumping into her body, and that other Japanese soldiers were kicking her ruthlessly into uncon-sciousness. By the time David Davis, hearing the commotion, had left his wife's side and raced to the women's courtyard, Gladys was lying unconscious on the ground.

David Davis stared aghast. There were at least thirty armed Japanese, intent on rape, with struggling, screaming, half-dressed women. Unarmed against thirty soldiers, David knew he stood little chance of preventing this outrage.

"Pray!" he bellowed to the women at the top of his voice. "Pray, all of you!"

The Japanese officer swung on him savagely and drew his revolver. From point-blank range he leveled it at David and pulled the trigger. David heard a click as the hammer fell, more clicks as the officer jerked the trigger viciously. Whether all rounds misfired, whether the pistol was faulty or unloaded, David will never know, but no explosion came. Cursing, the officer reversed his grip on the revolver, and with the butt hit David full force across the mouth. The im-pact knocked David Davis down; his cheek and mouth were slashed open. Groggily, he got to his knees, blood dripping down his shirt. He could taste the warm saltiness as he opened his lips again and shouted: "Pray! Pray, all of you!"

And now the women and girls were all down on their knees, their hands clasped together, praying loudly. The Japanese soldiers stared stupidly, not knowing what to do. The officer yelled at them, but they stood there sullenly.

159

Then he shouted a second order, and the soldiers turned away and shambled out of the courtyard. The officer stalked after them. A woman ran and closed the door; most of the girls wept with relief.

The women carried Gladys back to her room and revived her with cold water. She got up next morning, feeling bruised and sick. For many months afterward, she suffered internal aches and pains. But she did not let this interfere with her work.

While David was away, she continued to visit Yangcheng and all the small Christian communities she had started. The Chinese calendar, in the isolated mountain villages, did not include a Sunday, so that at each village, with its six-day week, the day when she arrived was declared the Sabbath. Hymns were sung and prayers offered up. Some villages, deep in the high mountains, had suffered little change in their manner of living. Scant news of the war penetrated to them. In the places near Tsechow, people lived in preparation for flight, their bundles around them.

In the spring there was heavy fighting around Tsechow. The Nationalists threw in large forces, and the Japanese, assailed on every supply route and in every village, pulled back from Tsechow toward Luan. Nationalist troops entered the city. It was two or three weeks later that the Bible Woman, Chung Ru-mai, came running into the Mission to tell Gladys that four important men were asking to see her.

"Who are they?" Gladys demanded. She remembered David Davis's warning that, at all costs, the neutrality of the Mission must be preserved.

"They're from the Nationalists," said the Bible Woman.

"Well, send them away; they can't come in here."

The Bible Woman went off, to return a few minutes later with the information that they still wanted to see her.

"You'll have to talk to them," she said. "They want somewhere to stay."

"If they think they can stay in our mission, they're mad!" said Gladys.

"They're important people," said Chung Ru-mai.

"Oh, are they? We'll soon see about that." She hurried out of the door to find them.

The four men in civilian clothes were standing in the compound outside the Mission door. They were young, and in some indefinable way different from all the other men she had met during her stay in China. They bowed, greeting her with the polite ceremony that is a part of any civilized Chinese meeting. "I'm sorry," she said, "but you can't come in here. This is a mission compound and we must observe our neutrality. You'll have to leave at once."

The leader of the party was a young Chinese with a dignity rather like that of the Mandarin. About his upright figure and unsmiling face was an authority she had not met before.

"We are sorry to cause you trouble," he said. "We thought you might help us."

She frowned at him. "How can I help you? You're fighting a war. This land belongs to God. Will you please leave?"

As his companions turned away, the young man inclined his head slightly. Gladys noticed the dark, shining hair brushed up from the high, pale forehead, the dark almond-shaped eyes under black eyebrows, the clear, golden skin, ears set close to a well-shaped head.

The other three men were already moving toward the compound door. He said quietly, "We are sorry to offend you, but when we were in Chungking, the Generalissimo said, 'If you want someone you can trust, go to the Christian Church.'"

She looked at him sharply then. "What have you to do with the Generalissimo?"

"We are his representatives. We believed that you would be on the side of China."

There was a gentle rebuke in his calm voice which slightly disconcerted her. She hesitated for a second, then said, "Perhaps you'd better come in and talk to me. But leave the other three behind."

He smiled. "Thank you." The others disappeared through the gate.

Seated opposite her in the Mission, he told her that his name was Colonel Linnan and that they were members of Generalissimo Chiang Kai-shek's intelligence service. The situation in Shansi was confused, and they had been sent to find out what was happening. It was an area vital to the defense of China. If they could blunt the prongs of the Japanese attack anywhere, it would be here, where the terrain gave little help to a better-equipped adversary, where lines of communication were easy to cut, and where, at the foot of the peaks, flowed the mighty barrier of the Yellow River. "The cost of mountain conquest," he said, "can be made prohibitive by small forces of determined men, properly placed." As he explained these theories in his pure Mandarin, he stared at her with his dark brown eyes. At the end he said, quite simply: "Will you help China?"

She had not expected such a plain question. "I'm Chinese —a naturalized Chinese," she said slowly, hesitating, trying to choose her words, "and I care deeply what happens to this country."

"Does God insist on neutrality in all things?" he asked gently. "Is he not against evil?"

"Yes . . . but . . ." It was most unlike her to be hesitant.

"Japanese intentions in China are evil, are they not?" he

162

continued. "China is fighting to the death in an effort to prevent this evil spreading. China *must* win this war."

Gladys hated the Japanese, but the hatred was not motivated by patriotism. It was odd that this gentle-voiced young man should force her to confront these issues. At length she compromised by saying, "I will help you as far as my conscience will allow me."

"That is most kind of you," Linnan said softly. "I will call again and talk with you further, if I may."

She went with him to the gate of the compound, then walked thoughtfully back to the Mission. It was strange; she had lived in such a rough, rude society that she had forgotten that anyone could be as gentle and charming as this young man. In fact, she had almost forgotten the existence of men in relation to women.

It was a week before he called again. The Japanese had been driven even farther back toward Luan, and large Nationalist forces were now grouped around Tsechow. The Chinese general and his staff had set up their headquarters in the city. Linnan came to see if his men could attend services at the Mission. She said she would be glad if they did. Several Japanese Christians, she told him, had attended the services when their forces had occupied the city. She noticed his eyebrows lift, saw the quick, angry dart of his eyes. She felt her color rising.

"That is what I came to China for, to preach the Gospel of Christ," she said sharply.

He inclined his head in a small bow; it was a constant gesture of his, and there was a dignity and apology attached to the action which never failed to soothe her indignation. He asked her many questions. He told her about himself; he had been educated at Peking and at the Central Military Academy in Nanking. He had traveled all over China, and above all he yearned for a China strong and free and incorruptible. He stood up then, almost as if afraid that he had talked too much. As he bowed good-by to her, and asked if he might come and talk to her again, she became aware, through some indefinable nuance of his speech, that he had called to see *her* personally. The thought came to her very suddenly, and it disturbed her. When he had gone, she went across to the cracked mirror in the corner of her room and stared at herself. She was thirty-five. Her eyes were large and dark, and although her skin was tanned by the sun, the years had chiseled only a few faint lines at their corners. But how somber was the dark blue, highnecked blouse. Unthinkingly, she plucked a white flower from a vase in a corner and stuck it in her hair. She found herself looking forward to his next call with an odd stirring of interest.

He came the evening before she was setting off for three isolated villages deep in the mountains, a lonely and difficult trek. She laughed and told him about it, wondering why he seemed perturbed as she described her route.

"Aren't there bandits in those mountains?" he asked.

"Yet, lots of bandits!"

"And you must travel alone?"

"But I usually travel alone."

"It must be very dangerous, and the passes are high and steep. If you fell and injured yourself, you could lie there for days and no one would ever find you."

Gladys looked at him, puzzled. In all the years she had been in China, no one had ever professed the slightest concern for her personal safety. Now this charming, good-looking young man seemed seriously worried. It was very unusual, but she decided she liked it.

"I shall be all right," she said. "I am capable of looking after myself."

"Please take care," he said. "Please take care."

She was a week out in the mountain country, and when she got back Linnan was waiting for her. His relief was quite plain.

"But I've made these journeys a hundred times," protested Gladys. "There's really nothing to worry about at all." That a young colonel of Chiang Kai-shek's Intelligence should be bothered about someone as inconsequential as Ai-weh-deh amused her; it was also very flattering.

His visits became more and more regular. They became good friends. They were the same age; both had eager, inquisitive minds. In the evenings they would often walk through the narrow streets of Tsechow, past the dark bazaars hung with Chinese lanterns, past the fortunetellers and the storytellers, the food stalls and the silk merchants' shops, among the gossiping and laughing soldiers. They would walk in the fields around the old walled city, and see the moon setting behind the tall temples and tiled pagodas. Linnan talked to her about China: its traditions and culture, its beauty and its spirit. He opened for her a new window on a country she had thought she already knew intimately but which she now realized she hardly knew at all.

Each time they met, in the weeks that followed, the immense gulf between their separate worlds grew narrower. His voice fascinated her; she had grown so used to the harsh mountain dialect that his musical flowing Mandarin was an endless delight. One evening, as he rose to leave, he bowed as usual, but his eyes in the soft lamplight held an awareness, an intimacy she had not seen before. She said good night abruptly. Was she attractive, she wondered? Was there still in her face and body the indefinable mystery that draws a man to a woman? She was a missionary dedicated to God. But God had also made her a woman full of the natural tides and forces which stir womankind. If she was falling in love, she reasoned, then it was God who allowed it to happen.

She had returned from a long trip into the mountains when the other thing arose. In two of the villages she had found Japanese troops billeted. She had paid small attention to their presence and had gone about her business, ignoring them. She told Linnan about it when she returned. He was very much interested and questioned her closely about the number of the troops, what weapons they had, where they were situated.

The next time she went into territory occupied by the Japanese she made more careful note of their numbers and their armaments, knowing that her reports would please him. He had stirred in her a latent patriotism for her adopted country and now, after these months, she almost was as fervent a patriot as he. It was a subject so closely allied to her evangelistic zeal that she wondered why she had never felt it before. The idea of a new, noble China rising out of the rubble of war, out of the debris of a corrupt, inefficient, and outworn society, was a topic of endless stimulation to them. She came to believe implicitly that anything that could hasten the defeat of the Japanese, quicken the molding of a new country, built upon Christianity, with a better society for the poor and the deprived, was of paramount importance. If she could spy for the Nationalist troops, bring back information of military value, pass through the Japanese lines unhindered and unwatched, and so help to defeat the common enemy, then she would do these things. How much of this activity was due to her desire to please Linnan, and how much to a desire to serve China, she did not try to disentangle. She knew only that in the bitterness of this war she was now equipped with a faith, and also a purpose.

166

CHAPTER TWELVE

WHEN DAVID DAVIS returned to Tsechow, both he and his wife, Jean, noticed a difference in Gladys. They both knew and liked Linnan, and welcomed his frequent visits to the Mission; but it never occurred to them that his companionship was responsible for Gladys's new happiness. Indeed, David thought he detected a hint of hysteria in her laughter. She had been working too hard, and ought to rest.

"What you need," he said seriously, "is a holiday, a rest cure. And I know just the place for you. At Lingchuang the Christians are holding a small conference next week. Why don't you go and help them? There's been little bombing there and, as far as I know, no fighting. It's an odd little town like Yangcheng. You'll like it."

Gladys smiled to herself. Lately she found she was often smiling to herself. She agreed to go. She was perfectly aware by now that she was deeply in love—with a love which was an intimacy of the senses more potent than any physical encounter. And because she had never been in love before, and had never expected to be, and because for ten years she had labored diligently for her Christian God, eating the mountain food, drinking cold stream water, sleeping on hard brick *k'angs,* resolutely disciplining her thin body to the hard work and the long days, this sense of mental and physical well-being was an intoxication of the spirit. She did not think God would grudge her this small holiday of her affections. She set off for Lingchuang feeling very happy.

167

With her went the Bible Woman, Chung Ru-mai, Timothy and Sualan. They loaded their possessions onto a small, two-wheeled, mule-drawn cart—the roads around Tsechow made the use of such a vehicle possible—and set off across the plain.

Late that afternoon, with the sun already dipping rapidly toward the mountain peaks, and Lingchuang only three or four miles away, they heard the familiar sound which had so often presaged death and destruction. They saw the silver planes droning down from the hot, haze-hidden sky, heard the scream of the bombs and the dull, ground-shaking thuds. They could do nothing but watch anxiously. Timothy and Sualan, climbing a little way up the mountain to get a better view, shouted excitedly. The Bible Woman and Gladys regarded each other with serious faces. The Japanese were bombing Lingchuang. The war had arrived. So much for the rest cure!

Gladys urged the mule forward. It was dark when they reached the city. The damage was not as bad as they had expected. Even at Lingchuang, people had learned to take shelter in a cellar or beside a wall when bombers came over. The Christian mission was undamaged except for a few shattered windows. Undaunted by the bombing, people from surrounding villages were already arriving for the religious conference, and next day the usual work of instruction began. Each day, at practically the same hour, the Japanese planes flew over and the bombs fell. The work of Christian instruction was interrupted again and again by the necessity of burying the dead and comforting the living, but the conference went on. Then, late on what was to be its last night, a strange rumor reached them: an unknown army was approaching the town. Japanese? Bandit? Communist? No one seemed to know. Gladys suspected it would be Japanese. Daily bombings before troops entered a city were usual with them. The conference was over anyway, and people prepared to leave. It was one thing to live in a Japanese-occupied town, but quite another to be in residence when a victorious army first arrived; far better to be in the mountains at such a time. The village Elders, for it was mainly of these that the conference consisted, decided to leave at dawn the next day. Everyone lay down to rest, baggage close at hand, but though Gladys turned and shifted position, sleep eluded her. Full of foreboding, she decided that they must leave Lingchuang at first light. She did not want a repetition of what had happened at Chin Shui; they *must* be out early. Eventually, unable to stand it any longer, she got up and aroused the Bible Woman, Timothy and Sualan.

"We're leaving," she said. "We're leaving straight away!" The others did not protest; they were used to her sudden whims and fancies by now.

Her voice awoke an evangelist from Tsechow who had come to the conference with his wife and two children. Overhearing the whispered conversation, he looked up with anxious, inquisitive eyes.

"You can't get out; the city gates will still be locked. They won't open them until dawn."

"Then we shall be first out," she said firmly. "Come on Sualan, Timothy, pack your things together."

Two other men from near-by villages, who were lying on the floor a few yards away, were also disturbed by the movements. They sat up. "We'll come with you, too," one of them mumbled.

Their decision obviously influenced the evangelist. He prodded his wife awake. His sleepy-eyed children sat up and looked reproachfully at Gladys.

"It may be a false alarm," she said, "but I've got a feeling I want to be the first through those gates when they open."

"It is three hours, at least, before dawn," protested the evangelist.

Gladys drew a deep breath. "I can't explain it, but I know we're going to be the first out," she said firmly. "There's no need for you to come unless you want to."

By the time the party filed out into the dark, chilly streets, it had grown by the addition of a young Chinese doctor, his old mother, his wife and baby. They had been visiting relatives in Lingchuang, and being Christians, had sought shelter at the Mission when the bombing started. The streets were empty. Timothy's cough echoed eerily. They reached the massive gate with its green-tiled eaves, curving upward at the corners, and paused in the black shadow. As the villagers had warned, the gate was locked. They crouched in a small huddle in the roadway against the heavy woodwork. Between the roofs behind them they could see the bright stars. It was cold and quiet; no lights showed in the city. The children quickly fell asleep again. The adults dozed off. Only Gladys kept awake. She put out her hand and touched the rough texture of the gate. It was wooden and solid, built to withstand any attack that the ancient town-dweller could visualize. She wondered vaguely why this desire to leave the city had so suddenly seized her. Would it not have been better if she had let them all sleep longer? After all, there had been no confirmation of the approach of an enemy. The Mandarin had made no official statement. No one had been warned to leave. It was purely her own intuition. Oh, well, she had to be satisfied with that.

The warmth of her padded jacket, the dark security of the wooden gate against her back, must have lulled her into a doze. She was awakened by the sound of the cocks shrieking that dawn was near. She opened her eyes. It was getting light and the gateman was busy with his locks and bolts, grumbling querulously at the human cargo in his way. A large crowd of people filled the roadway behind them, all anxious to leave the city as soon as the gates opened. The massive gates swung back on their hinges. A murmur of appreciation rose as the road leading to the mountains was revealed. The children laughed. They had not expected such excitement. The road stretched ahead of them, three miles of flattish country flanked by wheat fields before the track rose abruptly into the shelter of the craggy peaks.

Gladys felt her heart lighten as they marched along. A steady stream of refugees was moving out of the city gates behind them, and the sun shot golden light through the notched ridges of the mountains. They were perhaps a mile from the city when they saw the stream of refugees falling back on both sides, and for one moment of panic Gladys thought the enemy was among them. Then she saw that the horsemen galloping toward the mountains were Chinese cavalry, the pride of the Nationalist armies. They were a fine sight: a full squadron in gray uniforms and peaked caps, stirrups rattling, saddle leathers creaking, swords bumping as they pounded along. They were grouped in squadron formation, about twenty horsemen galloping together, then a space of about thirty yards, and another group. The children screeched with delight as the horsemen galloped past, raising a cloud of dust, the drumming hoofs making the earth tremble. Gladys wondered why the faces of the cavalrymen were so grim and intent.

Then suddenly she knew! Above the pounding of the hoofs on the baked earth came a shrill, insistent noise. Into that moment of fear screamed the high-pitched, hysterical sound of diving aircraft. For a fraction of a second her muscles refused to act. Then she screamed at the children.

"Into the fields. Run, run! Into the fields! Throw your-

selves flat!" She cuffed and slapped Timothy and Sualan over
the low stone wall that bordered the road, driving them frantically into the wheat field like cattle, yelling fiendishly at
them, as above the roaring engines came the metallic stutter
of machine guns. She threw herself down, covering her head
with her arms as much to shut out the horror of the scene as
to protect herself. The earth was churned. Horses screamed
horribly. There was a great shout of agony as the planes
roared along the column of refugees and horsemen, scything
them with bullets. Spotting aircraft had obviously noted the
Chinese cavalry as they approached Lingchuang the evening
before, to camp there for the night. Any military mind
could foresee that they would seek the shelter of the mountains at first light.

The planes came in over the mountains, zoomed down
upon the city and roared along the line of cavalry and refugees. Dead and dying refugees, troopers and horses collapsed
like puppets with the wires suddenly released. They choked
the road. Riderless horses, heads thrown high, eyes bloodshot, leaped the low wall and crashed through the wheat
field. The shrieks and the panic were more terrible than anything Gladys had heard before. Over the city and along the
road of twisted bodies the planes roared again and again.
Then the silver planes turned in a wide circle to examine
the carnage, and droned away, dwindling to invisible specks
in the sky.

She stood up, trembling. From the road and the fields, littered with dead and wounded, came groans. All around, the
bits and pieces of household possessions lay scattered in the
wheat. Horses limped or galloped aimlessly across the nightmare scene. Timothy and Sualan clutched at her jacket, saying nothing. The two villagers, the evangelist, the doctor
and woman looked expectantly toward her. They were numb

also. This sudden carnage had frozen their resolution, even their instinct for self-preservation. Looking back along the road, they could see the corpses of horses and humans around the city gate, choking the exit. Every impulse in Gladys's mind told her to fly to the mountains, to leave this ghastly battlefield and hide in the deep gorges away from the frightfulness. She stood mute. There were hundreds of wounded here.

She turned to the Chinese doctor, a thin young man, his scraggy neck pinched by a tight collar. But he looked terrified, for he had only just completed his training, and had no experience for an emergency such as this. Then, to the two villagers and the evangelist, she said: "You will take the women and children on to the mountains. Wait for us there. The doctor and I will stay here to help. We'll join you this evening." She looked at the doctor as she spoke. He nodded nervously. The women and children scrambled their few possessions together and hurried off. Gladys waved them good-by, and with the young doctor turned and hurried back toward the gateway. As they walked, she gathered every un-injured man, exhorting, threatening and scolding, in an attempt to muster a party to clear the gate. Dazed and blank faced, most of them followed her. Some, weeping beside the bodies of their dead, could not be cajoled into moving.

They reached the gate. Gladys, her spirit back now that she had a task to do, ran around shrilling instructions to her helpers. They heaved aside the bodies until a passageway was cleared. Then, with the doctor, she began to do what she could to help the wounded. Soldiers who were unhurt or only slightly wounded lent a hand. In the late afternoon other soldiers arrived to help clear the mess. At this point, having done all she could, Gladys and the doctor felt they could leave. The military were busy digging pits for the dead, heaving the belongings, the pitiful bundles and bags, into a heap for later sorting.

Numbed, bloodstained, exhausted, Gladys and the young doctor walked slowly toward the mountains. They were too tired to talk. As she stumbled along, Gladys found tears running down her cheeks. Sheltering at a bend they found Chung Ru-mai; the doctor's wife and his mother; the evangelist, his wife and children; Timothy and Sualan. The two countrymen had been home and had returned. They had found their own people preparing to flee, and were about to rejoin them. Rumors and counter-rumors were everywhere. News of the carnage at Lingchuang had lit a powder train of panic. Fighting seemed to be going on everywhere. Gladys realized that, at that moment, the only safe place was in the mountains far from any town or village.

It was not an unusual course to take; over the past two years she had spent many nights in the open or sheltering in caves. Among them, they carried enough grain to last for several days. After a short conference, the others agreed. In fact, there was little else to do; if this was a big Japanese offensive, the five towns, Tsechow, Yangcheng, Chin Shui, Kaoping and Lingchuang, would soon be in their hands.

Weary and sick at heart, the little party moved off the road and up through the mountains. They walked until it was dark and then crouched under a rock. Next morning at daybreak they set off again. Most of the time the old lady grumbled and moaned; they were all suffering from shock. Even the tall mountains, craggy and silent, with narrow gorges and high, bare faces, gave them no sense of security. All that day they picked their way deep into the mountains; in the afternoon they discovered a large, dry cave halfway up a steep slope. The children and the women were very tired and had no wish to go farther, and black thunderclouds were massing overhead, filling the sky between the peaks with an ominous purple gloom. As they crept into the cave, the storm broke and rain lashed down. Sitting crouched inside, her arms around her knees, tired and miserable, Gladys watched the rain falling outside. On impulse she took the iron cooking pot she had carried with her and let the water trickle into it. There were dried sticks in the cave, and animal dung. She broke up the sticks and piled them between the two low rocks. They blazed fiercely when she lit them and the pot of water perched between the two rocks was soon boiling. She tipped coarse twig tea into the water, and in a few seconds they were all gathered around, sipping the steaming, aromatic liquid from their bowls. They added more sticks to the fire; in the gathering gloom their shadows licked at the roof and walls of the cave, and their feeling of security slowly returned. In a second cooking pot, Gladys boiled their ration of millet, and they washed down the hot porridge with more cups of scalding tea. Food and drink in their bellies, a feeling of contentment seeped through them. Now they were weary; by the firelight, as the darkness grew, and the rain poured down with increasing fury, they lay down and slept on the warm sandy floor of the cave.

For six weeks they lived in that cave, sleeping on beds of dried rushes collected from the valley. The nearest supply of water was five miles away, but they saw in that factor an added safeguard. Just beyond the well lay a village where they bought eggs and grain. Their appearance caused no comment; refugees were commonplace by now. Their chief fear was of the wolves which roamed the mountains; practically every night wolves prowled outside the cave, and Gladys, the doctor, and the evangelist took turns keeping watch. Usually a well-flung stone was enough to scare them away. If necessary, they would light the fire and watch the green, glinting eyes back away to a safe distance.

Back in Lingchuang, Linnan was concerned in a drama about which Gladys knew nothing. The Japanese had been defeated in their efforts to follow up their bombing of the cavalry and the city was still in Nationalist hands. When Linnan heard of the disaster, he had hurried to Lingchuang. He knew Gladys had been visiting the mission there, yet he had received no message from her. All they could tell him was that she had left at dawn on the morning of the attack and had not been seen since. As he was colonel in charge of Intelligence in the area, it was the duty of his men to sort the debris of the battle. On the second morning after his arrival in Lingchuang, a hymnbook was brought to him for examination. The soldiers, who did not know what it was, had picked it up in a cornfield. Linnan recognized it instantly as belonging to Gladys.

Frantically, he went around questioning the soldiers who had buried the dead. As far as they could remember, they had not buried a foreigner. On two occasions, when the soldiers were doubtful as to who lay in certain graves, he ordered them reopened. Then, with no sign of her body, and remembering her predilection for the wild mountains, he sent messengers to the surrounding villages asking for news of her. At every opportunity, he searched for her himself.

They had been sheltering in the cave for almost three weeks, and Gladys was enjoying the feeling of security and peace. Often, because the old lady and the other woman talked or grumbled too much, she would climb out along the valley, find a sheltered spot in the sun and read her Bible, hour after hour. One afternoon, when she was seated comfortably on a rock a mile away from the cave, and quite alone, she was suddenly conscious of movement near her. She looked up, startled, and saw a farmer's boy of about fifteen or sixteen. He wore a straw hat, a torn blue jacket and trousers. Over his arm was a small basket containing half a dozen eggs. She was immediately on the alert. He stood there staring at her.

"Who are you?" she snapped.

It was a second or two before his lips moved. "I'm selling these eggs," he said. Gladys's eyes narrowed at such an obvious lie.

"Why are you selling them here?" she said sharply.

He stared at her stupidly. "I don't know."

"You don't wander across the mountains trying to sell eggs," she said suspiciously. "Do you?"

His eyes dropped. He shifted uncomfortably but said nothing.

"You can go back and tell whoever you're spying for that we're all here," she said angrily.

It could be that the local bandit leader, or a Communist group, had got wind of the strangers in the neighborhood, and this boy had been sent out to locate them. Probably they had offered some minor reward for information. She watched him clamber back up the mountains before she hurried back to the cave. The others listened to her story with dismay. It was then late afternoon.

"We must leave first thing tomorrow morning," she said, "and find a new place to hide."

When dawn came, she was impatient to be off, but the others dawdled. The old woman did not want to move at all, and said so. The doctor's wife had to nurse her baby. The evangelist's wife was slowly gathering her possessions together. At last Gladys could stand it no longer.

"Look," she said, "I'll go on ahead and wait for you at

the end of the valley. Please hurry." She pointed in the direction she intended to take, and set off with Timothy. She knew her departure might hurry them up a little, for neither the evangelist nor the doctor possessed any formidable qualities of leadership.

Gladys and Timothy reached the end of the valley and climbed a slight rise which led into the next. As they breasted the ridge, Gladys saw below a sight which caused her to come to an abrupt halt. Spread out across the valley and advancing toward them was a line of horsemen, obviously searching. To Gladys it meant but one thing; they were seeking her party. She said quickly to Timothy: "Run back and tell the others to go up the valley in the opposite direction. Tell them to go as far as they can, and hide."

Timothy's eyes were frightened. "But what about you?" he said anxiously.

"If they get me, they'll probably be satisfied," said Gladys. She saw the small boy hesitating. "Now go on! Do as I tell you, Timothy!"

She watched him run back down the valley, then she turned toward the horsemen and walked boldly in their direction. Still some distance from them, she shouted defiantly, "If it's me you want, here I am."

She knew the Communists usually shot first and established an identity afterward; but now all feeling of fear had left her. She felt only anger that they should have been betrayed by a small boy carrying a basket of eggs.

As her voice floated downwind, she saw the horseman in the center point with his hand and urge his mount into a trot and then into a gallop. As he clattered toward her she saw that he was a Chinese Nationalist officer. Only when he pulled up his horse in a flurry of dust and stamping hoofs a few yards from her, tossed the reins over its head, swung out of the saddle and raced toward her, did she realize it was Linnan.

She clung briefly in his arms. In an agitated voice he told her how he had briefed everyone he could find in the countryside to keep a lookout for her, offering a reward if they found her. The farmer's boy had brought back the information he needed.

They went on to the cave, finding the others about to leave; they gathered around laughing and chattering in relief. Linnan gave them the news: sporadic fighting was going on everywhere. For the present it was better that they should remain in the cave; they were safer there. He would arrange for food to be sent to them from time to time, and let them know when it was safe to return to Tsechow or Yangcheng. Ownership of both cities was being contested savagely at that very moment.

Indeed, during the next three weeks, Gladys and the children often climbed up a near-by mountain to see, in the distance, the Japanese aircraft swooping down to bomb Tsechow. But eventually it was the Japanese who were driven back, and when they did return to Tsechow it was still firmly in Chinese hands.

CHAPTER THIRTEEN

As SHE EXPECTED when she reached the mountain ridge, she could see the smoke of the Japanese cooking fires below. The pale blue smoke spiraled slowly upward against the clear evening sky. The enemy camp was hidden by a buttress of rock. She had done work like this many times through the summer months since leaving the mountains and returning to Tsechow. She held up her hand as a signal and the young Nationalist officer scrambled up onto the ridge beside her. His feet dislodged a few scraps of rock and she watched them pitch downward to where the line of soldiers crouched against the mountainside. Carefully the officer scanned the valley below.

"You say there's about fifty of them?" he said quickly.

"I counted them as carefully as I could this morning," said Gladys. "I don't think I'll be more than a few out."

"They'll be moving along the track toward Tsechow tomorrow at first light, that is certain," said the young officer eagerly.

"They've got sentries all around," said Gladys. "You'll have to be careful. One spotted me this morning as I crossed the ridge, but there was a valley in between. He couldn't do anything about it."

The man nodded. He was hardly listening any longer; his mind was automatically setting up the machine gun and placing his men to the best advantage along the valley so that no one would escape their fire. Gladys knew they would attack

180

at first light, pouring down from both sides into the natural bowl after the initial fusillade against the surprised Japanese. There were only thirty of them, but they were Northern troops, tall, fierce young men who fought with a bitter courage and hatred. They would tear into the Japanese and the battle would end in a bloody hand-to-hand encounter. The enemy would fight to the last man and be wiped out. The Chinese would suffer casualties, too. There would be blood on the valley floor, bodies littering the rocks.

"You will go back now," said the officer, turning to her again. "You led us well, Ai-weh-deh."

"Yes, I'll go back now," she said wearily. She had been walking since dawn. At first light she had left the little Christian community in Po Rem, a remote village in the mountains, and set off toward Yangcheng. On her journey she had seen the Japanese troops picking their way carefully along the dry river bed. She had known at once that they were very foolish to be so few in number, and so deep in the mountains. She knew where to find Nationalist troops. She had detoured from her route and entered one of their camps, well hidden in the mountains. At her news an officer and thirty men were quickly detached to accompany her; she had an army authorization signed by the resident Chinese general in Tsechow, but it was usually unnecessary to show it: the leaders of most units of the Nationalist army in that part of Shansi knew her very well. She knew the mountains in that area far better than most of the people who lived there, certainly far better than the troops. Years of wandering over the ridges and through the valleys on foot or mule-back, far from any habitation, had given her an expert knowledge of the terrain.

There were no set positions in this kind of warfare. The Japanese occupied the towns and tried to progress in force along recognizable lines of communication. The Nationalists, living in the mountains, adopted guerrilla and scorched-earth tactics.

With her Bible, Gladys moved through villages sometimes occupied by the Japanese, sometimes by the Nationalists. If they knew she was in their territory, the enemy ignored her; to them, she was no different from the thousands of refugees wandering around the countryside. They were unaware that she took careful notice of their dispositions, that she passed this information back to the Nationalist troops, and even led them to where she knew the enemy would be. She knew exactly what she was doing and was not ashamed of her actions. She was Chinese by adoption. Had she been in London, and England were in danger, she would have acted in the same way. Her heart had reached the fighting stage, even though she could not entirely quiet her conscience.

It was almost dark when she returned to the village where she had first met the Nationalist troops. The village Elder met her outside his house—a gentle old man in a faded blue robe, a straggle of white hairs on his chin. "General Ley is here," he whispered. "He called to see me; he is an old friend. When he heard you might return, he waited. He is anxious to meet you."

She quickened her step. She had heard much of General Ley, but had never met him. He was a legendary figure in the province, a Roman Catholic priest, a European, though from what country he came she did not know. In these days you did not ask questions about anyone's background. She heard later that he was a Dutchman, but never obtained confirmation.

When the Japanese invaded Shansi he had not been content to sit back and rely upon God's mercy. With militant Christian fury he had found weapons for his parishioners and struck back; now he was leader of a large guerrilla force. They lived in the mountains and fought the Japanese whenever and wherever they could. It was, therefore, with a tingle of anticipation that Gladys walked into the courtyard to meet this man who had managed to reconcile contemporary reality with his Christian conscience.

In the half light she saw him standing there, feet astride, arms clasped behind his back, a sturdy figure of medium height, dressed in a long black robe. His short cropped hair was blond; he had a strong, supple face; his mouth was determined, yet ready to smile. Only his eyes, she thought, were sad, detached. He smiled, hand outstretched.

"Ai-weh-deh! We shall forget that you are a woman and I am a man, that you're a Protestant and I'm a Roman Catholic."

"We seem to have some things in common, General Ley," she said, returning his smile.

"We have a common enemy," he said, suddenly somber again. His eyes were grave. "Come inside and let us talk. You must be tired and hungry."

As they scooped at their bowls of millet by the light of the flickering lamp, there was immediately between them that sense of warm friendship which so rarely illumines a first meeting. They talked of many things.

The main body of Ley's men were sheltering in caves some miles away. They were moving across to ambush the main trail between Tsechow and Kaoping the next day. Their information was good.

"We shall kill many Japanese," he said in a flat voice. "We have a machine gun. We shall cut them down as they pass." Hearing him speak and listening to the weariness in his voice, Gladys easily divined his inner despair. The same conflict existed in her own heart. "We shall kill many Japanese," he had said unemotionally—not as an ordinary military commander might have announced, "We shall cut their lines of communication!" or: "We shall capture supplies!" or: "We shall hit them hard!" He had gone straight to the heart of the matter.

"We shall kill many Japanese," he repeated. Their eyes met across the lamp. She understood, and he knew she understood, this agonizing dilemma of his Christian conscience. She, too, in the quietness of her prayers, had tried to find some clear path to follow.

Should he—should they—stand aside and let the forces of evil reach with black fingers into every corner of the province? Or should they take up the sword and, in the name of God, strike at the evil hand wherever it clutched? The policy of the Japanese was plain. For years they had ruled as a "master race" in their colony of Korea. They considered themselves aristocrats, the Koreans serfs. No Korean was educated above an elementary level; no Korean ever held an administrative post of any importance; they were reduced to a proletarian and peasant level and kept there. Hitler was putting the same theories into effect on the other side of the world. The same treatment was already being accorded to those areas of North China now in the enemy's grasp.

General Ley, the young Roman Catholic priest alone in his isolated Mission in southern Shansi, had had to make his decision in consultation with his own conscience and his God. He had gathered his flock in the courtyard of the Mission one clear, cold morning, and said, "We shall fight the enemy with the only weapon he understands. Force! We shall kill him when he sleeps, and when he is off guard. We shall drive him out of our mountains, no matter what the cost."

His men, mainly his own converts, Northerners, mountain people, their faces bronzed, their muscles hardened by their activity, an hereditary strain of banditry latent in their blood, were attached to him with a fanatical and ferocious devotion. He trained them in the arts of warfare. They struck with devastating speed, killed Japanese, captured supplies and arms, and retreated quickly into their mountains. This they had been doing for many months.

He sat on the rough brick *k'ang* in the Elder's house and looked at her across the table. The corner of his mouth turned up ironically as he spoke. "A common cause—eh, Ai-weh-deh?"

She scraped the last few grains of millet from the bottom of the bowl.

"General Ley," she mused. "Why do they call you 'General'?"

"The rank is purely honorary," he said, smiling again. "The men prefer it that way. They have more face serving under a general. And it is a convenient nom de plume."

She hesitated. "Aren't you frightened of being caught by the Japanese?" She knew it was a naïve question, but it was one she had to ask.

"Often," he said. "Very often. Are you?"

"I hardly think about it."

"I have heard much about you, Ai-weh-deh," he said quietly.

"What have you heard?"

"At times you make journeys behind the Japanese lines to gather information for the Chinese armies. That is true, is it not?" There was a ring of accusation in his voice, and she looked at him wonderingly.

"Yes," she said.

His eyes were fastened on hers. "Do you not feel that you

185

are betraying the position that God has given you?" he demanded coldly.

"I don't understand." She looked at him in bewilderment, anger slowly rising. Then her words burst out.

"God recognizes the difference between right and wrong," she said stormily. "We can recognize the difference, can't we? The Japanese are wicked. Our Lord drove the money-lenders out of the Temple with whips. The Japanese sweep through our countryside looting, burning and killing. We must drive them out, too, with every means in our power. These are my people they kill—my people legally, morally, spiritually—and I shall go on doing what I can to protect and help them. . . ."

She stopped suddenly in the middle of her tirade, conscious that he was smiling. "You did that on purpose," she said accusingly. Nevertheless she felt relieved.

He nodded slowly. "Yes." He paused and she heard his breath expelled in a heavy sigh. "We ask ourselves these questions, Ai-weh-deh, do we not? And even though we answer them to our own satisfaction, even though we can clear our conscience at any man-made inquisition, we are still not quite certain how we would answer at the court of God, are we, Ai-weh-deh?"

She did not answer. She knew he did not need an answer. He was examining his own conscience aloud.

"I am a Christian priest," he said slowly. "I am in this country to teach the ignorant and aid the sick, and bring the word of God to those who have never heard of it. And yet on the battlefield I see the corpses of the men I have helped to kill—yes, killed myself with these own two hands," he jerked out his hands in a quick gesture of contempt. "Yet what is the use of neutrality? There is fighting in every part of the world, Ai-weh-deh, against a common enemy of evil, and unless every man takes up arms—spiritual, moral and physical arms—and fights in the way he is best equipped to fight, how can we ever defeat it? I am a man as well as a priest, Ai-weh-deh, a man! You know what they have done, Ai-weh-deh, how they have killed and looted and burned and raped. How can a Christian man stand by while it continues? I cannot, and I shall not!"

Then, as quickly as it had risen, the anger died in him. He looked down at the hands still stretched before him, dropped them to his side, and wiped the palms against his gown with a downward movement as if to wipe out a stain. "The judgment must come later," he said wearily. His eyes lifted again after a moment of silence. A wry smile twisted his lips. "Mine is a religious order that believes in confession," he said quietly.

Gladys returned his look. "I understand," she said gently.

She did not know what else to say, although she yearned for words that would reveal her sympathy, and seal the bond between them. There was no way she knew of offering him comfort, beyond that his faith offered him. No one else could carry, or share, his burden. Yet she also knew that from this meeting between them, two aliens far from their homelands, each would take some comfort. In this way their meeting was endowed with dignity and a strength that neither would forget. She did not know that in the years to follow, in every latitude, such transient, comforting meetings of men and women for a few seconds, minutes, hours or days, were to be commonplace—that the old fabric of long, growing years, slowly ripening acquaintanceships, civilizing codes of conduct, was to be slashed to pieces by the exigencies of war. The few poignant moments before the battle, before the gas chamber, before the take-off, before the embarkation leave, before the surgical operation, before the falling bomb, were all that millions of men and women were to have as solace on their short and bitter journeys to the grave. Yet, in these little meetings of kindred spirits, without a past to give them guidance or a future to give them hope, they would find a measure of peace and coherence to lend a reason to their dying, a faith to give some semblance of sanity to the farcical affairs of mankind. Man, in all his wild adventures, had not, as yet, discovered a substitute for faith.

The wick burned low in the earthenware lamp. In the darkness General Ley left the house of the village Elder, and with his long black gown flapping about his legs, climbed back through the mountains to rejoin his men.

Gladys met him twice after that, but there were others present, and there was never time to do more than smile and exchange a greeting. It was many months later, in Tsechow, that she heard of his death. He had been killed by Chinese, the report said, but both Nationalists and Communists disclaimed responsibility. He would answer well at his "court of God," Gladys decided sadly.

The Chinese clung grimly to the territory around Tsechow through the autumn and winter and into the early spring of 1940. It was during this period that Gladys became friendly with the Chinese general based in the city. Introduced by Linnan, she was made welcome at his house; after several of her exploits, he personally gave her the badge which established her identity with troops in the field. She often dined with him and his officers. He was an older man than Linnan, with a long and honorable battle record behind him. He had been present as a junior officer at the famous Shanghai Incident when, on the night of January 28, 1932, the Japanese had sent companies of marines marching across the boundary of the International

Settlement of Shanghai and into the Chinese quarter, Chapei. He had been an officer of the Nineteenth Route Army which, with bitter gallantry, had so bloodily repulsed them. It was because of this unexpected resistance that Admiral Shiozawa of the Imperial Japanese Navy had sent in bombers to assist his marines, an action which created worldwide horror, for Chapei was a civilian city.

The General smiled ironically as he recounted the incident to Gladys. "It is surprising how acquiescent the world's conscience can become when an action becomes commonplace, is it not?" He was a wise and kindly man, considerate of his troops and contemptuous of the graft, corruption and greed that existed among his superiors in the Kuomintang.

It was for Gladys a period of fluctuating and feverish activity. David Davis had left the previous autumn to take his wife and children, and one or two other remaining Europeans, out to the coast; without his help they would certainly not have got through safely. Gladys knew he would be back as soon as he could. She spent her time both in Yangcheng and Bei Chai Chuang, roamed the countryside visiting her small communities of Christians, and in her travels amassed intelligence for the Chinese.

Few love affairs can have flourished in circumstances stranger than that of Gladys and Linnan. They met at odd moments in the mountains, in shattered villages, in bombed towns. They talked at odd moments between battles and births and baptisms. They exchanged scraps of news, had a meal together, talked of the future they would build in the new China. His concern, his gentleness, his tenderness toward her never wavered. They discussed marriage; he was eager that they should marry at once, live together as man and wife as best they could, war or no war. It was Gladys who said, "No." The war had to be won first. Marriage, their personal happiness, must wait. She wrote to her family in faraway England and told them that she was going to marry a Chinese, and hoped that they would understand. Her father wrote back and said that if her happiness would be secure with this man, they would be happy also. She read the letter in a cave in the mountains not far from Yangcheng, where she had been visiting some of her converts. How the letter had come up across the Yellow River and reached her in the mountains she could not imagine, but a messenger had brought it from Yangcheng. She wept a little as she read it, for all she had had to eat that day was a bowl of boiled green weeds plucked from the mountain side, and she was perhaps a little lightheaded.

With the coming of spring, every day brought the Japanese closer to Tsechow. They wanted that town very badly. In the fields and villages a few miles outside, the Chinese troops resisted them valiantly. A stream of wounded were passed back into Tsechow; even the compound of the Mission was used as a dressing station. Often Gladys went out with the bearers to bring in wounded men; they used doors torn from their hinges as stretchers.

Refugees streamed through the city and crowded into the Mission. The Japanese, steadily bringing up reinforcements, were applying heavy pressure. The noise of rifle and artillery fire was continuous.

In spite of all this, she was determined not to leave the city. She had lived so often under Japanese occupation that she felt she might protect her people from some of the worst excesses of their troops. She was worried about the children, however. From its inception, the Tsechow Mission had always cared for orphans; there had been between fifty and a hundred in residence even in normal times, but the number had grown enormously during the past few months. Now, there were over two hundred to be looked after.

She had known for some time that Madame Chiang Kai-shek had started a fund for war orphans, far away in Chung-king. Orphans were collected from war-ravaged areas, sent to the ancient capital of Sian, in Shensi, and there fed, clothed and sheltered. They were even given some schooling. During the winter Gladys had written to the authorities in Chungking asking if they could help her. She foresaw, after the stiff Chinese resistance of the past summer and autumn, that the Japanese would not be in a pleasant mood when they re-entered Tsechow, and she feared for the children.

A month later she got a reply. If the children could be brought to Sian, the committee would gladly look after them. She decided that half of them must go at once. She briefed Tsin Pen-kuang, a convert, for the journey. With money and supplies he set off with a hundred children for the Yellow River, where they would cross and catch the railway to Sian. Their journey was uneventful, and five weeks later she heard that they had arrived safely. She also learned that Tsin Pen-kuang was returning so that he could convoy the remaining hundred children to Sian. With conditions at the Mission becoming more and more chaotic, she eagerly awaited his arrival. She did not know, and would not know until months later, that on the return journey he was captured by the Japanese and presumably shot.

The morning that David Davis returned, she was on her knees beside a wounded man in the Mission compound, a bowl of hot water by her side. She heard David's voice behind her and recognized it at once. She turned and tried to smile a welcome, but found it impossible. Her thoughts translated themselves into words she would rather not have spoken.

"Oh, David, why did you have to come back now? It's so dangerous!" she said. Even as she spoke, she knew that nothing on earth could have prevented his returning to the place where he felt his duty lay. Now that he had evacuated his wife and children and the last remaining Europeans in Tsechow, and taken them on the long journey to the coast, the Mission was his concern. At the port of Chefoo he had left them in comparative safety in Japanese-occupied territory, and applied for permission to return to Tsechow. It had been refused. Undaunted, he applied for permission to visit a town a short distance from Chefoo. This he received. He had decided that, come what might, he was going back to his Mission. He set off with his pass to the neighboring town, and "disappeared." He knew the Chinese people, and ways of living off the country. He avoided the main routes where he might find Japanese and traveled "black" across country. It was more than a thousand miles and it took him almost two months by a circuitous route, walking every yard of the way.

He arrived to find his Mission packed with refugees and wounded soldiers, with a Japanese division attacking only a few miles away, and confusion everywhere. There was no time for Gladys to do more than exchange a few words with him; time was important, for she had decided that, at all costs, the remaining hundred children must be moved to safety. She was arranging that they should move back to Yangcheng that very day. With a couple of women mission workers in charge, she lined them up in a long column, made a rough check that they all carried their bedding rolls, basins and chopsticks, and saw them out of the Mission gate —a long procession of singing, chattering children headed across the plain, bound for the mountains and the safety of Yangcheng.

Young Murray Davis, son of David and Jean Davis, poses with Chinese Nationalist soldiers and refugee children.

At the compound in Tsechow: Gladys Aylward *(front right)* with David and Jean Davis and Chinese elders.

Gladys Aylward with some of the children before their epic march across the mountains to Sian.

Boys at Sian, recovered from their nightmare journey.

That evening she held a small prayer meeting in the Mission chapel. It broke up quite early, but she noticed one
young soldier—soldiers often attended the services—reluctant
to go. He stood in the doorway fidgeting with his cap. She
knew him quite well; he worked as an orderly on the General's staff. He was a youngster, shy and sincere.

"You're not in a hurry tonight," she said jocularly, as she
went to close the door and see him out.

"I had to wait until the others had gone," he said mysteri-
ously. "I have a message from the General." He produced an
envelope from his breast pocket and handed it to her. She
frowned, tore it open, and scanned the simple sheet of rough
paper. It was written by the Adjutant on behalf of the
General.

"The Chinese forces in Tsechow are on the point of re-
treating. The General would like you to accompany the
Army, who will take you to safety. If you go with this orderly
he will provide you with a horse, and lead you to a rendez-
vous."

Her expression grew even more severe. For some reason
the letter angered her. It was presumptuous of the General
to think that, at the first sight of danger, she would bolt for
safety. She had been in danger many times during the past
years. Although David had returned and the responsibility
for the Mission was now nominally his, she still felt that her
duty demanded her presence in Tsechow. She grabbed the
orderly's pencil and scribbled on the back of the letter, *Chi
Tao Tu Pu Twai*, "Christians never retreat!" She knew it
was a rather extravagant gesture, but it relieved her annoy-
ance.

"Take that back to your General," she said. He hesitated,

then saluted, turned on his heel and strode off into the darkness.

Gladys lay on her bed and thought about the letter. So the Japanese were going to take the city? Well, she had lived under occupation before, and could do so again. There was still so much work to do—so much work to do! Fully dressed, for in those days of alarms and counteralarms you never knew what the night might bring, she fell asleep.

It was the following afternoon that the orderly appeared again, his pale, thin face wearing a worried look. Gladys had just finished her midday meal of millet, and over her empty bowl she stared at him in astonishment.

"What have you come back for?" she asked.

He was flustered, agitated, stammering in his excitement. "The General pleads with you to come to safety at once. He has sent me back with this message. The Army is camped fifteen *li* away on the plain. I beg of you, Ai-weh-deh, to accompany me."

His distress aroused a tiny feeling of uneasiness in her mind. She put down her bowl and stood up. "Thank you for coming to tell me this," she said, "but as I have already told you, I will not go with the Army, no matter what happens. If I stay in Tsechow, or if I go into the mountains, it makes no difference."

To her, this was quite logical. Although she might help the Nationalists with information, she still retained her very definite ideas about Christian proprieties.

She left him standing there and walked away to go on with her work. Those of the Chinese wounded who could not walk were being loaded onto carts to be taken out of the city, and the walking wounded hobbled after them. The Japanese had no time for wounded, their own or the Chinese. Their own dead they collected in piles and cremated. The

Chinese were convinced that the Japanese helped their own badly wounded men toward a Shinto heaven with a carefully placed bullet before quickly cremating them. To the Japanese, only the act of sending a small urn of ashes back to the homeland shrines seemed important. They tore the doors off the houses and the courtyard railings from the balconies to get wood for the pyres, and this utilitarian treatment of the dead shocked the Chinese violently. To them the dead should be revered. They believed that three souls belonged to the departed, one inhabiting the ancestral tablet, one the grave, and the third journeying out into the Unknown. More than ever they became convinced that they were fighting a nation of barbarians.

All that day the city of Tsechow was being evacuated. The Japanese had been thwarted for too long by the Chinese rearguard action to show any mercy toward those they suspected or disliked, and the city was by now almost deserted. Gladys had not had time to discuss the General's message even with David. She knew he would not leave the Mission until he was forced out of it. He, too, had lived under a Japanese occupation before and thought he could endure it.

While they were gulping down some food at their midday break, they exchanged a few sentences about the condition of the Mission, but there was no time for a long discussion. The Mission was packed with refugees; there must have been almost a thousand of them in the compound, and David was trying to instill some sort of order into the confusion.

For many days now the rattle of small arms and machine-gun fire, the duller thunder of mortars and heavy artillery, had punctuated every waking and sleeping moment. Suddenly, that evening, it ceased. It was late and many people were already sleeping, but the very silence was in some strange manner ominous, terrifying. Gladys opened her window—the windows in the Mission were made of glass, unlike her paper windows in Yangcheng—and looked out into the dark courtyard. The very darkness seemed to breathe uneasily. She was annoyed at her own uneasiness and fear.

"Why should you be frightened of silence?" she asked herself. "Supposing the Japanese do arrive. They *will* come; you know that. What about it? You've lived under their occupation before."

But she knew also that she was opposing her intuition—the quick, vital instinct that had served her so well in the past. Her instinct made her uneasy, as nervous as a deer drinking at a night pool, lifting his head and scenting a tiger on the wind. She lay on her bed, fully dressed as usual, and closed her eyes. Weary from the long hours of organization and nursing, she dozed off. When the gravel rattled against her windowpane she awoke, startled.

She struggled up out of sleep, and got to the door. The wick of the castor-oil lamp still burning on the table gave a little illumination to the room. "Who's there?" she called sharply. She could not hear the reply but recognized the voice as that of the General's orderly. She unbolted the door. He stood there, a dark shadow against the lighter sky. His voice was agitated. "I have come to ask you to retreat with us at once, Ai-weh-deh," he said quickly.

Because she was a little frightened herself, her voice was irritable. "I've told you already I shall not retreat with the Army," she snapped. "Why do you have to bother me at this time of night?"

He did not attempt to come into the room but stood there, his voice full of appeal. "Whether you leave with us or not, you must leave. We have received certain information."

"What information?"

"The Japanese have put a price on your head."

196

"A price on my head!" She tried to laugh, but the laughter stuck in her throat. "What am I worth to anybody? The very idea's preposterous."

Without a word the orderly fumbled in his tunic pocket, produced a piece of paper, and handed it to her. "Those leaflets are being pasted up in the villages outside Tsechow. They will appear on the gates of this city tomorrow!"

She took it over to the lamp to read. The shadows danced across the small handbill, about eight by ten inches in size. Headed "One hundred dollars reward!" it continued: "One hundred dollars reward will be paid by the Japanese Army for information leading to the capture, alive, of any of the three people listed below."

Gladys's eyes scanned the names. First was the Mandarin of Tsechow; second was the name of a well-known business man noted for his Nationalist sympathies. The third line simply read: "The Small Woman, known as Ai-weh-deh."

CHAPTER FOURTEEN

HER IMMEDIATE REACTION was that the whole affair was unbelievable. A hundred dollars; it was a small fortune! "They must be mad!" she exclaimed. "Offering a hundred dollars for me!"

The dark figure in the doorway did not move. "You must leave by the morning, Ai-weh-deh. I go now. You must leave as soon as the sun rises."

Gladys turned back to him, undecided now, and unable to shake off a sudden sense of dread.

"Thank you for bringing me this news," she said slowly. "I'll decide something or other; I don't know what."

He detected the note of anxiety in her voice. "I wish you well, Ai-weh-deh," he said gravely. Then he was gone into the darkness; she never saw him again.

She closed the door slowly behind him and walked back to the table. She examined the small poster more carefully. A hundred dollars! It was a vast sum of money to most of the inhabitants of Tsechow. Without bitterness, she reflected that there were probably many among them who would betray her for half the sum. She did not think of consulting David Davis in her dilemma; for years now she had made her own decisions without help from anyone. She had not seen David for many months; and now that she was a woman with a price on her head, she did not want to involve him in her affairs.

The air in the room felt oppressive. She went to a window

and opened it. Darkness hung outside, thick and impenetrable; it was very quiet. "How can I run away in the face of the enemy?" she asked herself desperately, as another part of her mind warned her to seek safety at once.

Obviously the Japanese had learned of her intelligence work for the Nationalists. Someone had betrayed her. The enemy would have no scruples in squaring the account; nor would her sex offer protection. Yet she was still reluctant to leave. Her training, her heart and her spirit were all against abandoning her post in the face of the enemy. Yet she had seen many dreadful things these past years; the enemy were not above practicing many of them on a Christian spy. Inside her head a little voice warned, "If you stay, you will surely die."

There was a Chinese prayer that she knew well: "If I must die, let me not be afraid of death, but let there be a meaning, oh God, to my dying." Would there be a meaning if she waited meekly for the Japanese to come and take her?

She did not know what to do, but on impulse reached out for her Bible. It lay on the table next to the leaflet. She flipped it open at random, then bent forward to read, in growing awe, the line of Chinese characters: *Flee ye, flee ye into the mountains! Dwell deeply in the hidden places because the King of Babylon has conceived a purpose against you!*

"The King of Babylon has conceived a purpose against you!" she repeated aloud wonderingly. If she wanted a sign, was this not it? *Flee ye, flee ye!* Yes, she knew now that she must leave at first light. She went to her little box in the corner and began to pull out all her papers and letters. They must be burned before she left. Not a scrap of evidence of any sort must remain. She was still busy when dawn came, but she had completed her task. The sun was up when she went down into the compound, carrying her Bible and the small leaflet. One of the Chinese Elders, a good Christian she had known for many years, was already taking a stroll in the sunlight. On impulse she held out the small square of paper to him. He took it, looked at it reflectively for a few moments, then lifted his eyes to her. His expression was grave. "You should be out," he said. "You should be away from here."

"I'm going now," she replied. "I'm on my way to ask the gateman to get my mule ready."

As she crossed the wide compound to the front gate, she could feel the warmth of the sun on her back. Her feet in her thin shoes kicked up tiny spurts of dust. Mao, the gateman, was peering through the small spyhole in the door when she reached him.

"Mao," she said, "I'm leaving at once. Will you get my mule ready, please?" His round, fat face turned slowly to meet hers. Usually he was grinning but now he looked serious. His tight, round black hat seemed to constrict his forehead.

"You must look outside the door," he said. "It would be dangerous to leave now."

Gladys stepped past him. She put her eye to the small hole. It gave a view of the road, which to the left swung back and was cut off from view by the compound wall but could be seen to the right where it rounded the city wall and entered the main gate. A party of Japanese soldiers were marching through the city gate. She stepped back from the peephole, fighting a sudden wave of panic. As she turned away, she saw that for some unknown reason the cook, Mesang, had followed her across the compound. "You should be gone, you should be gone!" he called loudly.

She looked at him without answering, too stunned to

speak. Then she turned and began to walk back across the compound, and as she walked the feeling of panic increased. Her feet moved more quickly, she broke into a trot, and then ran. The back gate was her objective, the back gate through which, by immemorial custom, they carried out the dead.

The way to it lay through the courtyard, past David's quarters. As she raced through, she suddenly remembered his presence. On impulse she stopped, scooped up a handful of gravel, and hurled it at the glass panes. In a second he was at the windows. He must have been dressing, because he was in his shirtsleeves. She could see his head and shoulders as he stared out at her. His voice came plainly. "You're afraid, Gladys? Why are you afraid?" Suddenly the blind panic had her in its grip again; without a word in reply, she ran for the back gate.

It was open, and she ran through. Outside lay the Strangers' Burying Ground, an open stretch dotted with grave mounds. Beyond was the shallow, grass-grown moat which encircled the city, and away to the right stretched a large field of green wheat, not fully grown but tall enough to hide her. All this she knew by heart, but as she dashed through the gate, she also knew immediately that she had made one bad error of judgment. Although the front gate was closer to the city entrance, the route of escape from the back gate was exposed to anyone advancing along the road for a much longer distance. On the road, behind the detachment of Japanese she had seen entering the city gate, were other companies marching at regulated intervals. She had raced right into their vision. The nearest body of troops was no more than a hundred yards away. She knew their propensity for firing first and checking identities afterward. Anyone who ran from them invited a fusillade. If their shots found the target, rarely did they bother to go out of their way to inspect the corpse, or the wounds their bullets had inflicted. But she could not stop herself now; she was committed to flight.

As she raced through the graveyard, she heard the soldiers shouting behind her; then she was conscious of the crack of rifles, the whine of bullets glancing off the rocks around her. There was a pain in her chest, sweat in her eyes, but the edge of the moat was only a few yards away. She tried to hurry toward it, but, almost on the brink, she felt a blow on her back. Instead of running, she was suddenly flat on her face, with the dust and grit in her mouth. She felt no pain, only an intense surprise. She knew a bullet had hit her somewhere.

"I'm dying," she thought. "So this is dying?" Then she became aware of a burning sensation across her shoulder blades, and, with a quick return to common sense, realized that she was not dying at all, but soon might be, for bullets were still kicking up fountains of dust and ricocheting from rocks all around her. The Japanese soldiers were using her prone figure for target practice. With intuitive reflex action, she reached up and tore open the cloth fastenings down the front of her heavily-padded coat. Her Bible had fallen with her; she could feel it pressing into her stomach beneath her. She wriggled out of her coat, sliding it down behind her like a sloughed skin; then, using the Bible as a sledge, she wormed her way forward, pushing with her toes and tearing at the earth with her hands. Panting, she reached the shallow moat and tumbled into it. Her back was burning. Her heart thumped, as she listened to a shower of bullets spattering the discarded coat as the soldiers readjusted their aim. It gave her impetus. Doubled up, she scuttled along the moat until she could see the wheat growing above her head. Carefully parting it, she burrowed among the pliable stalks, edging backward so that she could lift up the slender stems and leave no telltale route of crushed wheat behind her.

In the middle of the field she felt fairly safe. She was sorry she had lost her coat, for all she wore underneath was a thin cotton vest, and even in the bright sun she shivered. She could feel the sting of the surface wound across her back. The bullet had torn through her padded coat and skidded across the right shoulder blade. Her exploring fingers located a thin groove in her flesh, but it had bled little, so she was not worried. Her eyes were heavy, and she felt weak. She remembered that she had hardly slept at all the previous night. Birds sang in the bushes around the field and on the walls of the city. There was no other sound. It was quite peaceful. She curled up into a ball and yawned. Of a sudden, she felt tired, as if all will and enterprise had ebbed from her body. She closed her eyes.

She was surprised when she woke several hours later to find the sun high in the sky, and realized that she had fallen asleep. It seemed absurd, even foolhardy, to sleep in such a situation, and yet she was pleased because she felt so much better. She was frightened no longer. When darkness fell, she knew the Japanese would lock themselves inside the city. Therefore she had to wait until the sun set before she could make a break for the mountains. To occupy her time before dusk, she tunnelled through the wheat to the farther edge of the field. As soon as the shadows were deep enough to give her shelter she slipped out of the wheat. She glanced back at the city walls. Not a soul moved in any direction as she hurried across the undulating fields toward the mountains.

It took her two days to reach the Inn of Eight Happinesses and when she arrived she knew what she was going to do. As she picked her way up the rocky slopes, as the wind whipped her face on the ridges, as she stumbled down the steep inclines into the valleys, she examined all the courses which were left open to her. She arrived firmly at one decision.

She must go! She must leave this part of Shansi altogether. After the bitter fighting of the past few months, the Japanese would not be merciful toward anyone they suspected. If they knew she was still in the territory they might take hostages against her surrender. She thought of Hsi Lien, and his wife and children burned alive. Suppose they did that to her friends or her children? She could not bear even to contemplate that thought. She would take the children—all of them —across the mountains to Sian and find refuge there. That was her decision as she came down the narrow road to the Inn.

The children were overjoyed to see her. They crowded around in the courtyard, laughing and chattering. The two mission workers who had looked after them told her that they had begged grain from the Mandarin and all were well and fed. Gladys gathered them around her, a sea of brown, smiling, almond-eyed, dirty children, who knew her as their real, true and God-given mother.

"Ai-weh-deh!" they clamored. "Ai-weh-deh has come to look after us."

"Tonight," she said, "I want you all to go to bed early. Tomorrow we're going for a long walk across the mountains. A long, long walk!"

There was a burst of spontaneous cheering, A long walk to anywhere was an adventure.

"You must get up early and tie your bedding into a roll and take your bowls and chopsticks with you. Now off you go, all of you, and into bed early. Don't forget."

They disappeared into every hole and corner of the building and, as Gladys looked up sadly at the broken roof and the sagging balcony, she reflected that it was, indeed, almost all holes and corners. She sighed to herself and walked to the gate. Every house in the little street which led to the Inn was badly damaged. As she walked through the East Gate and along the main street which had been concerned with so many important happenings in her life, she felt a sense of overwhelming sadness for the derelict city. The steps of the *yamen* were deep in rubble. In the first courtyard she thought of the old splendor, the pomp and officialdom and all the ceremonial litter of thousands of years of courtly behavior which had preceded those early meetings with the Mandarin. Now there was only one guard at the door of a small chamber. He recognized Gladys, grinned at her, pushed open the Mandarin's door and yelled: "It is she!"

As she went inside, Gladys reflected that in the old days such informality would have cost him his head.

The Mandarin came forward to greet her. He wore a plain blue robe and a black skull cap. For a passing moment Gladys regretfully recalled all those wonderful gowns of scarlet and gold. Even his long, glossy pigtail was now cropped to a stubby queue. All Chinese males had done this on Nationalist orders, for the Japanese had found ingenious ways of torturing men with long queues. They thought it uproariously funny to hang a man by his own pigtail.

"Ai-weh-deh," he said gently, "it is good to see you."

"It is good to see you also, Mandarin," she replied. She looked at him carefully. He was older. Scholarship had not made those deep lines around his eyes and mouth. Like her, like all the Chinese people in southern Shansi, he had lived the past few years in an agony of doubt and fear. When the enemy came he fled the city, carried on his civic business as best he could from a mountain village. When they left his city, he returned to its ruins. Neither the Communists nor the Japanese had any time for Mandarins; his life was in perpetual danger. But he smiled at her and inquired of her health, and her parents' health, and was anxious to help her. He listened gravely as she told him what had happened and of her decision to try to reach Sian across the mountains with the children. She could see he was disturbed.

"I have heard that the Japanese armies are infiltrating through the mountain passes and have reached the Yellow River," he said. "You will have to cross their territory. It will be very dangerous."

"We shall stay away from all the known trails," she told him. "We shall follow paths that the Japanese will never find."

"With a *bei* of children?" In Chinese numerology a *bei* was a hundred; in actual fact, there were a few below that number.

"With a *bei* of children," she said firmly. "I dare not leave one behind."

"That is true," he said sadly. He paused for a second, "You have money, food for the journey?"

"Neither."

He smiled, then chuckled aloud. "You have a faculty for facing the formidable, Ai-weh-deh, with a certitude and calm which I have envied ever since you came to Yangcheng all those years ago."

"I've said it to you many times, Mandarin: 'God will provide.' Now you believe that, too?"

"On this occasion, at least, let the Mandarin of Yangcheng act as His agent. I can provide you with two *dhan* of millet, and two men to carry them for the first part of your journey. It will take you several weeks to reach Sian by the route you will have to travel. You understand that?"

"I know. I'm leaving at dawn tomorrow morning."

"May God help you," he said. "May the good fortune you deserve be yours."

They bowed low to each other; they were old friends saying farewell, and each wished to convey his innermost affection through something more than words. But it was impossible—and also unnecessary.

She went back to the Inn. The children were stacked in rows on the *k'angs* once used by the muleteers. From the broken balcony she looked up at the star-filled sky and the familiar mountains. She knew in her heart that she was leaving Yangcheng, if not for ever, then for a very long time. Her mind swept back to that day when she had first arrived, cheerfully ignorant of all that lay before her. So much work and toil, and yet so much happiness, had been compressed into those full and useful years; nothing could uproot or diminish those memories. She tried to console herself with the thought that there would be more work to do in Sian when she arrived, but it did not help very much.

She wondered how David was faring. Had she known what was about to happen to him, it is probable that she would have returned at once to Tsechow to try to be of some assistance. But she did not know. And it was to be many long years before she did know the full story of David Davis.

Two weeks after the Japanese occupied Tsechow they arrested him, and accused him of being a spy. Although it was precisely one year and four months before the Japanese declared war on the Allies and David Davis was theoretically, therefore, a neutral, it made no difference whatsoever in his treatment. A thousand miles inside China, theoretical scruples played small part in Japanese strategy. For some oriental reason known only to themselves, they were determined to make him admit he was a spy. Their methods were quite simple. They starved him, kept him without sleep, and beat him viciously at regular intervals.

Two of his Christian converts they tied to beams and tortured in an effort to induce them to declare that David Davis had conspired against the Japanese. Both refused to condemn him. Both, they killed. They were simple men; they could not understand why they were being tortured into confessing to an untruth, something which they knew, and the Japanese knew, was an untruth. They died keeping faith. The Japanese had no grounds for suspicion regarding David, but he was a European and a Christian, and they distrusted both.

Why had he come back to the Mission? Why had he allowed Chinese soldiers to frequent the Mission compound? Why had he spied for the Nationalists? Why? Why? Why? Day and night he was made to kneel facing a plain wall and, if he fell asleep, he was wakened every hour by blows. For three months this treatment continued. They did not weaken his spirit or his determination.

They knew about Gladys, but she was out of their reach. They had found a letter addressed to her by a certain journalist from an American news magazine. Many months earlier he had crossed the Yellow River and penetrated up into Shansi in search of material. Because he knew little of the language, and because the Nationalists were suspicious of him, he was eventually directed to Gladys. He wanted to know what was going on, who was fighting whom, if the Japanese were really committing atrocities. Gladys had helped him all she could. Months later he sent her a letter from Chungking, thanking her for her help in supplying him with details of Japanese atrocities. He had sent it to Tsechow. He might just as well have sent a death warrant. When it arrived, Gladys was away, and David was en route for Chefoo. The letter was placed on David's desk and, during some periodic cleaning-up, it fell from the top down between the desk and the wall. Neither Gladys nor David, in their destruction of all personal documents and letters, had located it. The Japanese, when they searched the Mission for a final time, did not make that mistake. As soon as it was thrust in front of David's nose, he realized that if they ever caught Gladys it was the end of her. He declared that he knew nothing of either the journalist or the letter, which was true. He had been a thousand miles away at the coast when the visit had been made. But the Japanese were having none of his protestations of innocence. It was further proof of his guilt, they asserted. After three months of interrogation he was moved to a jail at Taiyuan.

The inhuman treatment continued. He was placed in a steel cage with a concrete floor and concrete back wall, with twenty other prisoners. It was a few feet square. They were jammed together in a hot, stinking mess, with no means whatever of satisfying even the primary requirements of sanitation. Day and night an electric bulb glared down upon them. At dawn—they knew it was dawn because the warden would give a single order, "Kneel"—they would kneel, facing the wall. They would stay in that position for hours; if they moved or spoke they were savagely beaten. Then they would get an order, "Stand!" With heads bent, because the cell was too low for anyone to stand upright, they would crouch immobile. At night came the last order, "Lie down!" —and they would lie on the concrete floor in a packed, contorted row. Once every two or three days bowls of *kaoliang* or corn would be passed in, and a little water. The prisoners would cram it into their mouths with their fingers.

Every few days David Davis was taken out for questioning. He was told that if he admitted to being a spy he would

209

at once be given better quarters and better treatment. He refused. He knew that they were trying to drive him mad; he also knew that while he was sane they could never defeat him. His resolution was a coil of steel inside him; the harder they twisted with their pliers of torture the more the coil contracted, and it contracted into a fist of solid indestructible metal. Even in the depths of his deepest physical misery there was a kind of exaltation in his suffering. If the Japanese had understood even vaguely the great mystique of Christianity, which had produced an unending succession of martyrs since that Good Friday when Jesus Christ was nailed to the Cross, they might have known that they were wasting their efforts. There was a core in the spirit of this man from the mountains of Wales which no physical degradation could destroy. For six months, they kept him in this cell—filthy, lice-ridden, heaped together with those other pitiful fragments of humanity. He saw neither sun nor moon, nor knew the passing of night into day or day into darkness.

At length it was the Japanese who admitted defeat. He was transferred into another cell which held only three prisoners; he was accorded slightly better treatment. He spent that time converting one of his fellow prisoners to Christianity. Two years after he had been arrested he was sent to the coast to be repatriated as a civilian. There, while waiting for the last ship which was to take him homeward, he learned that his wife, Jean, and his children were in a near-by camp. Forsaking any chance of repatriation, he hurried to see them. The boat sailed without him. His small daughter was ill with whooping cough. A complication which happens no more than once in ten thousand times had set in. In a few hours, she was dead. He spent the rest of the war with Jean and the two boys in an internment camp.

Today, he lives at Ely, a suburb of Cardiff, in a small house, running his own church and parish. He carries scars on his face from his encounters with the Japanese. But no scars within the deeper regions of his mind and heart.

There is no malice or vengefulness in the soul of David Davis.

CHAPTER FIFTEEN

AT SUNUP the young children were up and shouting, running around the courtyard, throwing their bundles of bedding at each other, playing tag and generally behaving in the normal way of young children all over the world. With the aid of the older ones, Gladys tried to sort them out and feed them. There were nearly twenty big girls varying in age from thirteen to fifteen, Ninepence and Sualan among them. There were seven big boys aged between eleven and fifteen. The rest of the children varied from four to eight, wild, undisciplined, laughing, weeping, shouting little ones. In vain she tried to tell them that they must save their energy for the long day ahead; she might just as well have told a stream to stop running. The two coolies sent by the Mandarin, carrying their shoulder poles, a basket of millet suspended at each end, arrived at the front gate. Gladys said good-by to the two mission workers, to several other friends collected there; and after one last look around the broken inn, they were on their way, the children scampering ahead, dodging back through the gates of the city, shouting loudly that they could walk forever and ever.

They followed the main trail southward for several miles. Gladys had a whistle which she had obtained from a Japanese soldier months before, and she blew it occasionally to call the more adventurous little boys down from outcrops of rock and twice to line them all up in rows for a roll call to see that no one was missing.

They stopped by a stream to boil millet in the iron pot which Gladys carried; she heaped the steaming grain into the basins as each child came up in turn for its helping. At the end of this serving there wasn't much left in the pot for her, and from that moment onward that is the way things usually turned out. The children revived after the meal, began to clamber about the rocks again, and made excited forays ahead, to lie in wait and ambush the main party. She gave up trying to keep them in order. As the afternoon progressed, these minor expeditions became fewer and fewer, and soon she had four small ones hanging onto her coat, protesting that they were tired, and could they all go back to Yangcheng now? Gladys took turns with the older boys carrying them. She felt a little tired herself.

It was getting dark when they came to a mountain village she knew, and where she thought they might find shelter for the night. Not, she thought, that any householder would be particularly anxious to house a hundred noisy, dirty children. Help came from an unexpected quarter. An old Buddhist priest, in his bright saffron robes, stood on the steps of his temple as the Pied Piper of Yangcheng and her brood straggled past.

"Where are you going?" he called to Gladys.

"We are refugees on the way to Sian," she said.

He came down the steps and approached her, his small eyes almost lost in the maze of wrinkles and lines that creased his face.

"But what are you going to do with all these children, woman?" He sounded most disapproving.

"I'm looking for a place for us to sleep tonight."

"Then you can stay in the temple," he said abruptly. "All my brother priests are away. There is plenty of room. Tell them to come in. It will be warmer than the mountainside."

The children needed no prompting. This was something like an adventure! It was dark in the temple, and there were gloomy recesses in which stone figures of the fat, bland, heavy-lidded Buddha resided. There were painted panels depicting the many tortures of the Buddhist hell, but the children were too tired to notice them. They crowded around the iron pot when Gladys had finished cooking the millet, and when they had eaten, they curled up on their bedding and slept soundly.

She did not sleep so easily. For one thing, the temple was alive with rats, which squeaked in the darkness and ran over the sleeping children. A small, creeping doubt had entered her mind as to the wisdom of starting this journey with so many small ones. Perhaps she was overestimating her own ability. It was one thing to journey through the mountains alone, quite another to take a hundred children with you. The first day had been troublesome enough, yet all the children were fresh, and she was crossing country she knew intimately. The older girls had not complained, but she could see that several of them had suffered already. They were completely unused to mountain walking; the feet of several of them had once been bound, and even many years free from bindings were not enough to turn them into healthy limbs capable of withstanding the drag and scrape of the rocky paths.

For perhaps an hour the big boys tried to fight off the rats; then they also became too tired to persevere, and fell asleep. Gladys lay on the hard floor; above her head the impassive sculptured face of the stone Buddha was illumined by a shaft of moonlight streaming downward through some aperture high above. The more she thought about the future, the less she liked it, but there was no chance of retreat now; she had to go on.

The next day was a replica of the first. The children awoke refreshed, and with a complete lack of reverence began to explore the temple with shrill, admiring cries. The priest smiled urbanely; he did not seem to mind at all. He bowed when Gladys offered her thanks and wished her a safe journey to Sian.

They were far from any village when the next night caught them, and they huddled together in the shelter of a semi-circle of rocks out of the wind. In the night there was a heavy mist and the children huddled under their wet quilts, and next day their clothes steamed when the sun rose, and gradually dried out. That afternoon they met a man on a mule traveling in the same direction as themselves. If they would come to his village, he said, he would be glad to find them shelter for the night. Gladys accepted his offer gratefully. In his courtyard, the children spread themselves out and scooped cooked millet out of their bowls until their stomachs were full, then drank cupful after cupful of the hot twig tea. They still thought it all a wonderful adventure. Even Gladys felt an immense sense of relief with another day safely past, and the Yellow River one day closer. She cupped her bowl between her hands, embracing the tiny warmth it offered, and chatted with the older girls.

"How many days will it take us to reach the Yellow River, Ai-weh-deh?" asked Sualan, diffidently.

Although Gladys had never been through to the Yellow River, she knew the answer to that question well enough. "The muleteers on the regular track used to take five days. We're going right through the mountains. About twelve, I'd say."

"And we won't see a single Japanese soldier the whole way?" asked Ninepence.

"I hope not," she answered. She looked at the two girls

as they chatted, the girl she had bought for ninepence, and the slave girl from the *yamen*. They were both exquisite little creatures, with clear, pale skins and blue-black, shining hair. Even in their dusty padded coats their prettiness was unimpaired. She thought wistfully how beautiful they would look in the ceremonial robes of China, and wondered if they would ever know such luxury. How absurd that they should be forced to make this long journey to save their lives! She felt an unreasoning anger at the stupidity of all men, that they should be the cause of this ordeal. She yawned. It was odd, this constant tiredness. "Probably the added responsibility of the children," she thought to herself, as she wrapped herself in her bedding quilt and lay down to sleep.

In the morning the two carriers of the millet had to return to Yangcheng. They had reached the limit of their province. However, the man they had met in the mountains proved a good friend; he provided them with another coolie who would carry what was left of the millet until it was finished. Even with careful rationing, it did not look as if it would last another two days.

The next two nights were spent in the open. Two of the older boys, Teh and Liang, had obtained a pot of whitewash from a village along the way, and they went on ahead daubing a splash of white on the rocks to mark the trail across the mountains. Sometimes they would write a text across a rock: "This is the way. Walk ye in it!" or: "Fear ye not, little flock!" There were squeals of appreciation as the messages were translated to the young ones.

This was new country to Gladys but she knew they were heading south by the direction of the sun. They were thirsty practically all the time, for the sun was hot and wells were to be found only in the villages. After the heavy, wet moun-

216

tain mists each morning, they would gather around any drip from the rocks and moisten their tongues. The millet was used up now, and the carrier went back to his village. They had no more food and the mountains stretched ahead of them, wild and barren, with few places of habitation. Often, when they climbed over virgin rock, the slopes were so steep that they had to form a human chain down the mountain-side and pass the younger children down from hand to hand. They cried when they fell down, and cried when they got tired. Often Gladys tried to rally them with a hymn, and when they reached a level patch of ground they would all march bravely along, singing the chorus. The older children and Gladys were carrying practically all the bedding now, and often they would give one of the five- or six-year-olds a ride on their backs for a short distance. There was rarely any moment when a small hand was not clutching at Gladys's jacket.

Seven nights out from Yangcheng found them camped in the heart of a mountainous region unknown to her. They had found a small trail which led southward. It was not yet dark, but everyone was too exhausted to move farther. The thin, homemade cloth shoes which everyone wore were practically worn out. The big girls' feet were cut and bleeding. Everyone was filthy with dust and dirt. They had no food. Gladys raised her head to scan the party lying in huddled groups under the rocks. She did not like what she saw; unless they received food and help very soon, she was afraid of what might happen to them. Suddenly, she saw Teh and Liang, who were still acting as forward scouts, running back toward her. They were shouting something which she could not hear, but their obvious excitement presaged danger.

"Men!" they shouted. "Soldiers!"

Gladys froze in a moment of panic. She put her whistle

into her mouth to blow the prearranged signal for the children to scatter, but she did not blow it. If they scattered into this wild terrain they might all be lost and would starve or die of exposure in the wilderness. And then, as the boys stumbled toward her, she saw men in uniform rounding a buttress of rock down the valley, and with a gasping sigh of relief realized that they were Nationalist troops. The children had sighted them also. Their tiredness fell away and they bounded over the rocks to greet the newcomers. Gladys, with the girls, advanced more slowly, and as she walked suddenly heard the sound she dreaded more than any other. The noise of aircraft engines! With a thunder of sound that echoed through the valley, two Japanese fighter planes tore through a cleft in the mountains and hurtled over their heads. Although they must have been hundreds of feet up, their sudden appearance, the abrupt roar of their engines, sent a shock wave of panic through everyone.

She threw herself in the shelter of a rock, glimpsing from the corner of her eye that the girls were doing the same. She crouched, rigid, waiting for the rattle of machine guns. None came. She looked up, as the planes disappeared, catching sight of the stubby wings, the Rising Sun insignia painted on the fuselage. But the airmen were obviously intent on something more important than machine-gunning Nationalist troops or refugees in the mountains. Gladys stood up and looked down the valley. The children had been well trained in what to do in case of attack by aircraft. They were scrambling up from their hiding places. The Nationalist troops, who had also scattered wildly, were mixed up with the children. They rose from the rocks, laughing together.

There were about fifty soldiers, reinforcements from Honan passing up country to join a Nationalist force farther north. Gladys met the young officer in charge and explained their predicament, but the problem of the hungry children was being solved spontaneously. Soldiers were plunging their hands into knapsacks and producing treasures of sweet foods. All around Gladys could hear the delighted voices of the children. The soldiers decided to camp in that spot for the night. They invited Gladys and her brood to stay with them and share their food. It was a feast. They had foodstuffs not seen in Shansi for years. The children sat around the small fires, stuffing themselves to bursting point. Even Gladys, for the first time on the journey, ate her fill. When the troops moved on at dawn the children waved them a sorrowful good-by.

Each day now took on something of a nightmare tone. Strangely enough, the young children bore up well. They were used to little food; at night, no matter how hard the ground, they slept to a point of complete insensibility; and they woke refreshed and ready to play and gambol next morning. They charged up the mountains, lost their bowls and chopsticks, cried and protested, but they all remained healthy. Sualan, Ninepence, Lan Hsiang and the other girls were in a pitiful state. The sun had cracked their lips and burned their noses. Their feet were blistered and sore, and they could hobble only a few hundred yards before they had to rest again.

Nevertheless, no one gave up, and they moved slowly onward through the mountains. On the twelfth day they came out of the high country and down through the foothills toward the Yellow River. As usual at this time, the small children's voices were a constant background of complaint.

"Ai-weh-deh, my feet hurt!"

"Ai-weh-deh, I'm hungry!"

"Ai-weh-deh, when shall we stop for the night?"

"Ai-weh-deh, will you carry me?"

"Look down below," she said. "Look over there—the village of Yuan Chu, and beyond it, far away, look, the Yellow River! See it shining in the sunshine!"

"But it is so far away, Ai-weh-deh. And we're so hungry!"

"In the village of Yuan Chu they'll give us food, and then we'll arrive at the Yellow River. And when we cross that we'll all be safe. Now let's sing a song as we march down to the town."

No band of shipwrecked mariners looking from a raft with salt-bleared eyes at a friendly shore, no thirsty travelers in the desert beholding an oasis, looked more eagerly at that distant, shining ribbon of water than Gladys and the older children. The twelve days since they left Yangcheng had been long and weary ones; now at last they were in sight of relief.

They followed the road which led down from the foothills to the town. It had been badly bombed. Rubble littered the streets and most of the houses were roofless. There was an unaccountable silence about the place as they approached. No dogs ran yapping to meet them. No carriers or coolies moved in the streets. The children ran from house to house, their shrill voices echoing in the courtyards. There was no one there. It was deserted. Then Liang and Teh, the two older boys who acted as scouts, reported that they had found an old man. Gladys hurried up to him. He was sitting against a tree in the sunshine, a cone-shaped straw hat on his head, a few white hairs straggling from his chin. His thin legs stuck out from blue cotton trousers. He had been asleep and was querulous at being awakened.

"Old man, this is Yuan Chu, is it not?" she said loudly.

"Yes, this is Yuan Chu."

"But where are all the people. Why is the city deserted?"

"They've run away. The Japanese are coming and they've all run away."

A thin dribble of saliva ran down his chin. He was toothless and his face was shrunken to the bone.

"Why haven't you gone? Why are you still here?"

"I'm too old to run. I'll sleep here in the sun until the Japanese arrive, and if they kill me, who will care? All my sons are gone. All my family are broken like wheatstalks in the wind. I'll wait for the Japanese and spit at them."

"But where have all the people gone?"

"Across the Yellow River, away from the Japanese."

"Then we must go there, too. Are there boats?"

"There were boats once. Now I think you are to late." He cocked a rheumy old eye at the children crowding around him. "Where are all these children from? Where are they going?"

"We are refugees journeying to Sian," she said.

His lip curled contemptuously as he looked at her. "You are a fool woman to bother with all these children. The gods intended a woman to care for a handful of children, not an army."

Gladys had heard such philosophy in China before. It brushed over her head.

"How far is it to the river?"

"Three miles. Follow the road to the ferry, but you will not find a boat there. The Japanese are coming and they will not leave their boats to be captured. Go back to the mountains, woman. They are the only safe places!"

"We are going to Sian," she said quietly. She blew her whistle and the children lined up around her. It was Cheia's turn to be carried so she humped him on her back. "As soon as we get to the river we shall bathe and wash our clothes," she said. "And we shall catch a boat and be safe on the other side. Good-by, old man, and good luck!"

He did not turn his head to watch them go. He let it slump forward on his chest; he was asleep before they had turned the corner.

They trudged down the dusty path to the river edge. There were reeds along the bank, and little bays edged with sand where the children could splash and paddle in the shallows. They ran toward it, shouting and excited. The river was about a mile across, running swift and deep in the center. But there were no boats, and no sign of any boats!

Sualan said quietly, "Where are the boats, Ai-weh-deh?"

"They must come across every now and then," she answered. "Perhaps we're too late today. We'll spend the night here on the river bank, so we'll be ready to go aboard the boat first thing tomorrow morning."

They huddled together in a hollow on the bank. A moon rose above the Yellow River. It was very beautiful, but she had no eyes for its beauty. Birds rustled uneasily in the reeds and occasionally a fish would ripple and leap, the splash disturbing the silver surface. It was quiet and peaceful, but she was very much afraid. Where were the boats? Why were there no boats? Was the old man right? Had everyone fled across the river to avoid the Japanese? Were they trapped against this broad ribbon of water? She fell eventually into a deep but uneasy slumber, and dreamed that hordes of little yellow men in round, steel helmets, carrying a large flag, bright with the scarlet and white insignia of a rising sun, were marching closer and closer.

When she woke next morning the children were already playing in the shallows. The youngest were shouting: "Ai-weh-deh, we are hungry. When shall we have something to eat, Ai-weh-deh?"

"Soon," she called, "soon!"

She gathered the older boys around her. "We must look for food. Back in Yuan Chu, they must have left a few oddments of food. You must go and search the houses. Look everywhere. We must find a little food."

The children went on playing in the shallows. The boys trailed off to look for food in the deserted town of Yuan Chu. Gladys sat on the bank and watched the sun climbing up the sky, reflected blindingly in the surface of the wide river. She felt sick. The children had still not got over their amazement at the sight of so large a river, and they explored and poked in the reeds and the shallows along the banks. But curiosity would not fill their bellies for long. "If only a boat would come!" she thought. "If only a boat would come!"

Three hours later, the boys came back triumphant. They had scavenged through most of the houses in Yuan Chu and each bore some small contribution, a few pounds of moldy millet in the bottom of a rotting basket; a few dusty-looking, flat, hard cakes of dough, from under a shop counter. It was all boiled in the communal pot over a fire of dried reeds, and the result was ladled carefully into the forest of waving basins. There was not enough for Gladys or Sualan or the older boys, but the younger children were fed.

The sun rose high, and still no boat moved on the surface of the river. The boys went off to search for more food along the banks; there were a few scattered houses there. She sat quietly watching the children, half alert for the distant rifle fire that would herald the approach of the enemy. The boys came back with a few more scraps of food which she hoarded for the next day. That night the children huddled together on the bank of the river and whimpered before they went to sleep.

"Ai-weh-deh, we're hungry."

"Ah-weh-deh, when are we going to cross the river? When are we going to cross the river, Ai-weh-deh?"

She comforted them as best she could, and one by one they dropped off to sleep. The cold, white moon came up from the opposite bank and sat in the sky looking at them. A cold little wind rustled in the reeds with a thin dry rattle. Scarves of opalescent white mist hung above the surface. The water noises were soft, muted. Gladys lay on her back and looked up at the stars. Somehow, it was easier at night. In the sunshine the grim reality of that immense water barrier, the lack of food, the whimpering children, was a factual burden so heavy as to be almost insupportable. But at night the edges of the present and future were blurred—softened and eased by the slow falling of peace which preceded sleep. There were a few short hours of forgetfulness before the hot ball of the sun lifted above the horizon and the yelling swarm of children raced for the water to splash and shout and greet the dawn. And, besides, tomorrow it might all be different. Tomorrow, a boat might come.

They ate the last crumbs of food on the third day at the bank of the Yellow River. The sun rose and the children grew tired of racing along the banks. She told them stories and they sang songs together, and her eyes were sore from staring at the water in search of a boat. As the sun went down again, they crept close to her so that she could touch them with her hands. On the morning of the fourth day even the youngest children had caught the mood of despair. It was then that Sualan said:

"Ai-weh-deh, do you remember telling us how Moses took the children of Israel to the waters of the Red Sea? And how God commanded the water to open and the Israelites crossed in safety?"

Happy ending for "Ninepence," who is seen in Shanghai after her marriage, with her small son and "Grandmother" Aylward.

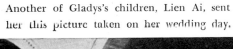

Another of Gladys's children, Lien Ai, sent her this picture taken on her wedding day.

The orphan "Less," one of the children who made the journey over the mountains, later sent his picture to Ai-weh-deh, inscribed: "Dear Mother, remember me. I am always yours with love." Soon afterward he and other students at Nanking University were shot by Communists.

Gladys Aylward shortly before leaving China after twenty years.

Today, with the same Bible which accompanied her on all her travels. Gladys Aylward still preaches throughout England.

"Yes, I remember," she said gently.

"Then why does not God open the waters of the Yellow River for us to cross?"

She looked wearily at the pretty, childish face, the ingenuous wide eyes. "I am not Moses, Sualan," she said.

"But God is always God, Ai-weh-deh. You have told us so a hundred times. If He is God He can open the river for us."

For a moment she did not know what to say. How to tell a hungry child on the banks of an immense and wide-flowing river that miracles were not just for the asking? How to say, perhaps we are not worthy of a miracle? How to say, although I can face a mortal enemy wherever he may beset me, I cannot open these vast waters? I have no power other than the power of my own faith.

She said: "Let you and I kneel down and pray, Sualan. And perhaps soon our prayers will be answered."

The Chinese Nationalist officer commanding the platoon scouting on the enemy's side of the river looked back at the column of soldiers straggling along behind him. They were boys, all of them, boys pressed from hinterland villages, with rifles shoved into their hands, and ill-fitting uniforms pushed onto their backs, quickly acquiring the ability to live off the land as an elementary part of their military and self-survival training. There were eight of them, unshaven, their heads closely cropped.

Oh, they would fight. If they ran into a probing Japanese patrol they would go to ground, and the bullets from their rifles would pick up tiny geysers of dust around the feet of the enemy. They would hold them for a while, unless the other patrol had a mortar, or unless they whistled up one of their fighter planes to spray them out of existence with cannon shells. They would hang on as best they could until nightfall, if possible. Nightfall would save them. Then they could signal their comrades on the far bank, and the precious boat camouflaged with reeds could be pushed out into the river and ferried across.

The young officer flicked a fly from his sweaty forehead and sucked in his breath. His wandering thoughts suddenly jarred to a standstill. A noise! An odd noise! A far-off, high-pitched sound, wavering and uncertain. A plane? His men thought so; he watched them thumb back their helmets and roll their eyes around the cloudless sky in an effort to locate it. There had been an unusual lack of air activity up and down the Yellow River for the past week. Usually the Jap planes patrolled and fired at anything that moved, even firing bursts into the reed beds at the sides of the river, and occasionally loosing off a sustained burst into the river itself so that a momentary barrier of furious water heaved up in a wall of hissing intimidation.

And yet this sounded almost like singing. Faint and far-away, high and monotonous, the sexless piping of many children. He shook his head as though to clear it. The river at this point was a mile wide; there might be children left in the villages on the other side of the river. Perhaps they were in a school; but would their voices carry this far? He mounted a slight rise in the bank, crawling carefully to the top. He raised himself to see better, and grunted in astonishment. He reached for his binoculars and focused. It was an astonishing sight. A great crowd of children were assembled on the bank, all seated in a circle and singing loudly. Some smaller ones were splashing and jumping in the shallows.

He motioned his men back with a hand signal. "Wait here," he said. "It may be a trick. Be alert."

The Japanese had driven refugees before them on many other occasions. And who were these children? All refugees had left this area days ago. The river was officially closed. As he walked along the bank, he could see that they were Chinese children all right. They saw him, the young ones, and raced toward him, gurgling and shouting with delight.

"Ai-weh-deh," they screamed, "here's a soldier. A soldier."

The young officer noticed, then, the small woman sitting on the ground. She was thin, hungry looking. She got to her feet as he approached, and with a shock of surprise he realized that she was a foreigner.

"Are you mad?" he said. "Who are you?"

"We are refugees trying to reach Sian," she said simply.

Her Chinese was excellent, though she spoke with the heavy dialect of the north. But although she was small like his own countrywomen, and her hair dark, he knew she was a foreigner.

"This will soon be a battlefield. Don't you realize that?" he said.

"All China is a battlefield," she said wearily.

"Are you in charge of these children?"

"Yes, I am in charge of them. We are trying to cross the river."

He looked at her directly. She was quite a young woman. Her dark hair was scraped back into a bun; her clothes were old and soiled; there were dark circles under her eyes, and her face had a sallow, unhealthy look.

"You are a foreigner?"

"Yes, I am a foreigner."

"For a foreigner you chose a strange occupation."

She looked steadily at him, and he said, "I think I can get you a boat. It will need three journeys to take you all across,

227

and it is dangerous. If a Japanese plane comes over when you are halfway across there will be little hope."

"We *must* cross the river."

"You will probably manage to get food in the village on the other side. The people do not like to leave their homes even when the Japanese come."

"I understand," she said. "It was like that with us in Yangcheng."

He walked to the river edge, inserted his fingers in his mouth and whistled loudly three times in a peculiar piercing way. From across the river came three answering whistles. Two little figures far off on the other bank pushed a boat into the water and began to scull it across.

"I cannot thank you enough," she said. "I thought it was the end of us when we couldn't cross the river."

The young officer saw her sway a little as one of the children pushed against her.

He looked at her curiously. "You are ill," he said. "You should find a doctor. The Nationalist troops on the other side of the river will have a doctor."

"I am all right," she said. "When we get to Sian I shall be all right."

With shouts of glee the children filled the boat. The soldiers ferried them rapidly to the other side. They returned and more of the children piled in. On the third journey the soldier helped the foreign woman into the boat with the last group of children. His platoon had gathered around to help. As the boat moved away from the bank, he called his men to attention and gravely saluted. He called: "Good luck, foreigner!"

He turned to walk back along the bank to his platoon. As he walked he looked into the sky, and listened for the drone of Japanese planes. None came. It was curious about that foreigner. If this had been close to a large city or a settlement, he could have understood it, but wandering across a battlefield escorting an army of ragged Chinese children—that was, indeed, very curious.

CHAPTER SIXTEEN

THEY FOUND A VILLAGE two or three miles from the bank of
the Yellow River and the people were hospitable to them.
Although many hundreds of refugees had passed through,
they still found food to spare for the children. The village
Elder apportioned so many to each house down the main
street, and when their initial hunger was appeased the children scampered from house to house to see how the others
were faring. Gladys heard their shrill questions. "What are
you eating in your house?" "We've got *bingsies,* what have
you got?" "We've got *mientiao.*" "Oh, rotten old *mientiao.*
You can keep it!" "But we've got rice cakes too, see!"

It was just as well, thought Gladys wearily, that they
didn't worry about where the next meal was coming from.

They stayed in the village only long enough to finish the
food, and then moved on. If the Japanese were approaching
the river, she wished to get as far away from it as possible.
They spent that night in the fields, and went on again next
morning to the town of Mien Chu. It, too, had been badly
bombed, but an old woman directed her to a refugee organization. She found it in the old temple; there were caldrons
of steaming food; they were made welcome. And then the
police arrived. The inspector was a fat, fussy little man bulg-
ing with a sense of his own dignity. He marched up to Gladys.

"I understand," he said, "that you say you have just
crossed the Yellow River."

"Yes."

"Then you are under arrest. You could not have crossed the Yellow River."

"Under arrest! But what for?"

"You say you crossed the Yellow River."

"Yes."

"No one else crossed with you?"

"No . . . only the children."

"If nobody else could get across, how did you get across?"

She shook her head in bewilderment. "We met a soldier who signaled for a boat."

"You could not have met a soldier who signaled for a boat. You could not have crossed the river. You are under arrest!" He pursed his lips seriously. This was obviously the most interesting crime that had been committed in his area for a long time.

"You didn't expect me to stay there and wait for the Japanese, did you?" she said heatedly. "And if you arrest me, you'll have to arrest all the children too."

A pucker of astonishment creased the bland, official face at this new complication.

"You mean to tell me you are in charge of all these children?"

"I am, and there's no one else to look after them." She was tired, it was late, and she wanted to rest. She tried wheedling.

"Why don't you leave us alone tonight? I'll come down to your *yamen,* or the police station, or wherever it is, first thing tomorrow morning, and you can arrest me then."

The fat policeman looked dubious. "I shall have to examine you before the Mandarin," he said importantly.

"Well, I shan't try to escape with all these children, shall I? I'll come down to the *yamen* tomorrow morning and you can ask all the questions you want."

231

He had to be satisfied with that. He went off into the growing darkness and Gladys wearily spread out her bedding; it appeared that escaping officialdom was almost as difficult as escaping from the Japanese.

Next morning, with the children, she went down to the *yamen* to be interrogated. The children were not allowed inside, and rumors that something awful was going to happen to Ai-weh-deh had spread among them. They stood in a block outside the front door, and as soon as she went inside they set up a chant which grew steadily in volume: "Let her out! Let her out! Let her out!"

The Mandarin was a benign-looking Elder who showed that he had little sympathy with the policeman. That official's evidence was both repetitive and absurd.

"You say you crossed the Yellow River?"

"Yes."

"I say you did not!"

"But I tell you we did," Gladys protested. "How could I have got from Shansi to Honan unless I crossed the river?"

"Then how could you have crossed without a boat?"

"We crossed in a boat! A soldier signaled for a boat!"

"Then you have committed a crime. You will please examine this document." From the hands of one of his orderlies he produced a massive and important-looking scroll, and handed it across.

Gladys scanned it. Among the seals and important looking hieroglyphics, she read that by decree of the general commanding the Nationalist armies in that region, the Yellow River was closed to all traffic. No one could cross it or journey upon it. The order was dated five days previously.

"So that's why there were no boats," said Gladys. "I wondered why."

"Do you admit now that you have committed this crime?" thundered the stout policeman.

"Of course I have," retorted Gladys angrily. "We are refugees from Shansi proceeding to Sian. There are a hundred children with me. You didn't expect us to wait on the other side to be killed, did you?"

Outside, the chant of the children went on monotonously: "Let her out! Let her out!" Now they had found the windows, and a dozen small faces were peering through, and they were tapping the panes with their fingers.

"Let her out! Let her out!"

The Mandarin had had enough. "It is plain," he said, "that if this woman has committed an offense it is of the smallest technical nature." He smiled at her. "If you can control your children for a few minutes, I think I may be able to help you."

She went outside. A few sharp words and a few indiscriminate cuffs got the children into order. She went back to see the Mandarin. The policeman had disappeared.

"Every morning," he said, "a train leaves Mien Chu and travels along the river in the direction of Sian. It does not reach there, because something has gone wrong with the line, but at least it will take you some distance on your journey."

"But we've no tickets, and no money for tickets," said Gladys.

He looked at her gravely. "In Honan today," he said, "all trains are refugee trains. No one is expected to have tickets. Tomorrow morning go to the station with your children and get on the train."

Gladys thanked him and took the children back to the refugee center. That afternoon she led them all to a pond on the edge of the city, and they tried to wash the worst of the dirt from their clothes and bodies. In the evening she assembled them in the courtyard and addressed them.

"You all know what a train is, don't you?" she said.

There was an excited babble of conversation. No, most of them didn't know what a train was. What was it? They'd never heard of such a thing.

Gladys demonstrated with sound effects, and "Oohs" and "Ahs!" of delighted anticipation greeted her description. Sualan, Ninepence, Teh, Liang, the older boys and girls, were, on the surface, more sophisticated about the approaching experience. Of course, *they* had heard about trains. What was there to get excited about? But they were excited, nevertheless.

"Tomorrow you will line up with clean hands and faces, and anyone with a dirty face or dirty hands will not be allowed on the train." Her speech over, the children scattered, to play about and terrorize the other refugees in the temple, before clambering into their bedding, chattering eagerly of the experience that was to befall them next day. They dropped off quickly into the sound sleep of the very young and very innocent, within minutes of wrapping their quilts around them.

They were all up at dawn next morning, eagerly tying up their bundles, scrambling to be first at the great stone basin full of water in the temple courtyard, so that faces and hands should be the color required by the omnipotent Ai-weh-deh. They lined up to have their basins filled with steaming millet, scooped the thick mixture into open mouths with dexterous chopsticks, and with astounding co-operation formed a long column, before Gladys had even tied up her own bedding.

She thanked the woman running the refugee center, blew her whistle, and with great laughs and cheers and an explosion of chatter, they set off for the train. The station was a long raised concrete platform three feet above the track. Any roof it had possessed had been blasted away long before by falling bombs. A hundred yards from the platform the railroad tracks curved out of sight between a jumble of houses. It was upon this bend, on being told that from this direction the train would appear, that a hundred pairs of eyes were focused.

Gladys had lined them up in three straggling ranks. The air was tense with anticipation, and after a few minutes, far off, there came the noise of the train! One hundred children tensed, a little uneasy. Those were very strange noises. Such whistling anger, such a terrifying rattle and hiss! Eyes twitched toward her and back to that fatal curve. Was Ai-weh-deh sure she was right about this "train" thing? Even in the distance it sounded like the grandfather of all the dragons in the world. Supposing it gobbled them all up? The noise grew greater. Couplings clanked as bumpers met, brakes screamed in steely anguish, and around the corner, steaming and blowing and snorting, came the hideous iron terror. There was one loud, anguished squeal of utter fright from the children. The ranks dissolved: panic was contagious. Bundles, basins, chopsticks flew into the air. Children fled in every direction. By the time the train was twenty-five yards away, not a single child remained on the platform. The wooden cars clattered to a halt. The engine subsided into heavy, steamy breathing and Gladys tried to collect her charges.

The older boys and girls, already ashamed of their sudden panic, were rounding up the younger ones, plaintively protesting that they had run away only to catch the others. One batch of eight-year-olds were found to have raced all the way back to the refugee center. Children were retrieved from under boxes and bales, from every conceivable hiding place within two hundred yards of the station. Group by group, Gladys assembled them once more on the platform. Fortunately the train seemed to be in no hurry to go anywhere at all. The cars were simply wooden boxes with roofs. There were no seats. And there were many other refugee passengers with their bundles and basins.

She managed to pile all the children into one long car, and when, an hour later, the train jogged slowly into motion, the children began to enjoy their experience.

There was only one other moment of panic. About two hours after they'd left, an elderly Chinese gentleman sitting a few yards from Gladys, and surrounded by children, carefully produced a stub of candle from his pocket. He placed it on the floor and tenderly lit it. At least three little boys immediately blew it out. At that moment the train plunged into a tunnel. The darkness was impenetrable, the wails and screams beyond description. The elderly gentleman, after a minute or two, succeeded in relighting the candle, and this time no little boy even breathed in its direction.

For four days they stayed aboard that train as it rattled forward in slow, short stages. Occasionally it stopped for hours, and all got off and stretched their legs. At intervals along the line, there were refugee feeding camps where they were given food and tea. Gladys dozed a great deal of the time. It wasn't that she felt ill; it was as if a general tiredness had settled into her bones. They had been almost three weeks on the road now, soaked by the rains and chilled by the winds. She had slept badly and gone without food for days on end. It was only to be expected, she told herself, that she shouldn't feel as well as normally.

At the small village of Tien Sha, the train stopped. It went no farther. An important bridge had been blown up, the tracks were destroyed. Here the undulating plain ended, and mountains rose steeply ahead of them. They had to cross these mountains on foot, then they would find more trains on the other side.

A thin stream of refugees moved up through the rocky passes: old men, young women, fathers, mothers, families laden with bundles, all fleeing westward away from the malison of the Japanese. They begged food in the village, and Gladys looked at the high peaks ahead. They frightened her. She didn't want to go on; she just wanted to stop where she was and rest. But she knew it was impossible. Their only hope was Madame Chiang Kai-shek's organization in Sian. Even though the city was still many days' journey away, somehow she had to summon up sufficient reserves of strength to get there. But those mountains! They looked so high and cruel. The sun sank behind them, and every valley and peak was suffused with its crimson glow. At any other time she would have admired the scene; now, she was afraid of what lay ahead. Next day they started on their journey again.

At first the trail ran upward. They were all practically barefoot, and the sharp flints cut their feet. Looking back from the first ridges they could see the dust rising slowly from the plain below, with the red ball of the sun glaring like a demon eye through the haze. For four hours they toiled upward, the youngsters scrambling ahead, Gladys and the older girls climbing more slowly. From a high shoulder of the mountains they had their last glimpse of the plain; then, as they dropped down, following the winding path, the peaks closed in on them.

Late in the afternoon Liang and Teh, the inevitable scouts, came back to report a village hidden in a turn of the valley ahead. When Gladys reached it, the children were already drinking basins of *mentang,* the water left after the

millet has been cooked, and the villagers were sharing rice
cakes and other odd fragments of food with them. She drank
some tea and felt better. The people were kindly. It would
take them two more days to cross the mountains and reach
Tungkuan, they told her. There were other villages on the
track where they might get food. Slowly, she struggled to
her feet. Another high ridge stood up against the skyline
in front of them. She reckoned that if they could cross that,
they could spend the night in the valley beyond. Another
hour's climbing, and the five-year-olds were already clinging.
Four of the fourteen-year-old boys took turns carrying them.
Gladys carried one also; the big girls were much too tired
and weak to help. It was all they could do to walk at all.
The progress of the entire party was very slow now.

The sun was sinking before they reached the ridge, and
Gladys realized that they could not cross it before dark. The
only thing was to find some sheltered spot and spend the
night. As on the previous night, the sun went down in the
same stupefying welter of crimson, and darkness came swiftly
out of the valleys. Under overhanging cliffs they found a
little shelter and huddled together, seeking warmth. The
younger ones were so tired that they were asleep as soon as
they were wrapped in their quilted bedding. It quickly grew
cold, and she could feel the chill striking through to her
bones. She wedged herself between two rocks and fell into a
deep, troubled sleep.

As soon as it was light, they wrapped up their bedding
and set off again, the youngsters tearing off ahead. They
crossed the ridge as the sun came up. All around were bare
peaks, stretching away in every direction, intimidating and
desolate. A chill little thought settled in her mind. If ever
they lost the track, they could wander until they died amid
such desolation. All that day they filed painfully onward.

It was in the afternoon, when they were seated on a rock for one of their frequent rests, that the breaking point was reached.

Her face streaked with lines where the sweat had coursed down the white mountain dust, Gladys stared around at the children. The eight- and nine-year-olds were still ahead, but two dozen of the little ones, with their mournful faces, the five- and six- and seven-year-olds, were gathered around her, almost too numb to plead to be carried or be given food or drink. The girls were slumped in attitudes of utter dejection on the rocks. Even Liang and Teh sat glumly, their chins in their hands, worn out by carrying the small ones for hour after hour.

It was then that Gladys felt something wet flowing down her cheek. She tried to brush the tears away, but they only came faster, faster and faster, and soon she was sobbing aloud, abandoning herself to grief, sobbing because she had no strength to stay her tears, sobbing from sheer weakness and exhaustion, sobbing for all the children, for all China, and all the world, so deep was her misery. At that moment she had no heart to go on any further. She was convinced that they were all finished; that they would all die in the mountains. She was convinced that she had brought them all to this plight, that she had betrayed them, and she wept because of her guilt. The children sobbed with her, and the little boys coming back down the trail stood openmouthed and then, influenced by the contagion of grief, began to wail also. For many minutes the sound of their distress echoed in the valley. When it was over, Gladys wiped her face with her coat sleeve and sniffed. The tears had washed away the bleak desperation, washed away even a little of the aching tiredness that weakened her will and her determination. She smiled wanly at Sualan, who crouched against her.

"A good cry is always good for you!" she said stoutly. "Now, that's enough, all of you. We'll sing a hymn, and while we're singing it, we shall march down the track to that big buttress of rock. So stand up, everybody, and no more crying. Let's see who can sing the loudest, shall we? One . . . two . . . three. . . ."

The mountains in their long years of sun and wind and rain must have seen many strange sights, but it is doubtful that they had seen anything more unusual, or more gallant, than this column of children led by a small woman with a tear-stained face, caroling with such shrill determination as she led her band onward toward the promised land.

Just before sunset they came upon another village and the kindly people ransacked their houses for food. The village Elder wagged his thin goatee at Gladys and said simply: "You have many mouths to feed, but who can resist you!"

They camped that night in a cave at the edge of the village, and the children, with a little food in their stomachs, slept as soundly as ever. The third day was a repetition of the others, except that they found no more villages and ate no more food; and that night, as they crouched on the mountainside, the mist was very heavy. The younger ones were asleep, but Gladys and the boys went around arranging basins to collect drops from the rocks, so that at least there would be a little to drink when they woke up.

Next day they came down through the mountains and onto the plain. It was still many miles to Tungkuan, but they got there just before dark. Most of the houses were in ruins, for the town had been badly bombed. A woman directed them to a courtyard where a refugee organization was to be found. Two women were in charge of the steaming pots, and the children clamored around them. A few—the inevitable few who were always losing their basins and chopsticks—clung to Gladys, wailing their dire distress to the world, and wearily she sorted things out and saw that they all had enough to eat. As usual, when all the children had been fed, there was only the pot scrapings for her. Not that she minded; she felt too tired for food. She discovered from the women that the railroad track ran from Tungkuan to Hua San, but no trains ran along it. The line passed too close to the river, since the Japanese occupied the opposite bank. That meant they would have to go on walking. The news irritated her almost beyond reason, and to be irritated was unlike her; she took most things in her stride. When two men came into the courtyard a little later and began to question her about where she had come from, and where she was making for, she answered them abruptly. When they pressed her, she snapped at them, "Oh, leave me alone, I'm tired!"

"We wish to help you," they said. "The women here have told us about you."

"How can you help me?"

"Every now and then a train *does* go through to Hua San, which is on the road to Sian. It carries no passengers, only coal. It starts in the middle of the night and it is still dark when it passes the Japanese positions on the other side of the river. Sometimes, however, they fire at it."

"You mean we might be able to go on it?" she said eagerly, her heart lifting at the news. "When does it leave?"

"Tonight, in a few hours."

She looked around at the rows of small bodies, wrapped up like cocoons and fast asleep. Not even an earthquake would wake them up. Her hopes receded.

"How far away is the station?"

"Round the corner, not more than seventy yards from here."

Her hopes lifted again. "If we could carry the children to the trucks and put them in, would that be all right?"

Yes, they would help as best they could. Excitedly Gladys called the bigger children together—Liang, Teh, Sualan, Ninepence, Timothy and Less. She explained what she intended to do. They were all to go to sleep at once and she would wake them when the time came. They would form a human chain down to the station: about five yards between each of them, and pass the young children down from person to person like fire buckets. Yes, just as they had done over the steep parts of the mountains.

The man smiled as she explained her plan. They would return when the train was ready, and tell her. She lay down and tried to sleep. She heard the soft breathing of the children all around her, such a soft, sighing rustle, and fell asleep herself. The next thing she knew someone was shaking her shoulder. The men had returned; the train would soon be starting; they must not waste time. She went around waking the older children. Everyone spoke in whispers, but even in the darkness she could sense their excitement. They spaced themselves out at intervals. The two men went down to the train to superintend the arrangement of the small, inert bodies on the coal trucks. As she lifted the first child, little San, a boy of five, she felt how light and yet how warm he was. He murmured in his sleep as she passed him to Sualan, and Sualan passed him on to Liang. She knew from experience that these children slept like hibernating squirrels and even if, inadvertently, they were dropped, they would curl up again on the ground and sleep on. One by one they were passed down to the train. Then Gladys rolled up the bedding into bundles and that, too, was passed down the line.

She went down to the train. She could hear the engine

242

wheezing, quietly somewhere up in the darkness, and she could see by the heaped-up silhouettes of the cars that they were, indeed, heavily laden with coal. The coal had been piled high above the sides of each car, the children placed between chunks of coal high in the air. The men had wedged more chunks around them to prevent them from falling off. She assigned two older children to each car, so that they could watch the young ones when they woke up.

She climbed up herself, grazing her knee on an iron stanchion. She felt the gritty surface under her hands. There were six small ones wedged on her car; they all seemed fairly safe. One of the men called out to her from below that he was going to tell the engineer that they were all aboard. A few minutes later the bumpers began to clank and the train moved forward in a series of jerks.

"Good-by, woman! Good luck!" the second man called from the darkness below.

"Good-by, friend," she called in reply. "Thank you for your help. And God bless you!"

The train picked up speed. The wind was cool on her face. Not cold like the mountain air, but softer and warmer. The stars were a bright canopy overhead. She lay back, her head against a chunk of coal. It was useless to think of dirt, but who would have thought that this black mineral buried a million years ago, mined from the deep earth, would prove such a good ally, if such a hard bed? She put out her hand and touched the smooth chunks of coal.

The wheels rattled and rumbled beneath her. There was exhilaration in her heart. What was the year? 1940? April, 1940, and here she was, rattling across China on an old coal train. She did not know that the Germans had broken through at Sedan and were pressing her countrymen back toward the defeat and glory of Dunkirk. She did not know that at that moment ships on every ocean were being blasted to matchwood. She did not know of the howling sirens that screamed around the blacked-out mansions in Belgrave Square like hungry wolves. She did not know that in America, in all the world without dictators, the great urge toward freedom was gathering strength and massing its forces.

None of this she knew. Only that she was content to lie on her coal car rattling along under the stars toward her distant goal, Sian. And presently she slept.

When she awoke, dawn was breaking. The children were waking also, and she could hear their delighted screams all along the cars. Little San, waking two feet away from Gladys, stared at Lufu rubbing his eyes, and screamed with laughter. "Lufu, you've gone black in the night!" And Lufu screamed back at him in happy and concerted agreement. "And you've gone black in the night, too. Ai-weh-deh's black! We've all gone black. Isn't it funny?" It was a concurrence of opinion which brought happy laughter in every car, and Gladys laughed with them.

The Japanese had not fired at the train, or if they had, she had not heard them. She felt refreshed, but weaker. They had left the yellow dust of northern Honan, and the river. Now they were passing across pretty, undulating country with orchards in full blossom and glimpses of pagoda roofs through heavy green trees, and the children exclaimed and pointed as each vista swung into view. They had seen nothing like this before in their lives. In the early afternoon they came to Hua San, one of the holy mountain shrines of China, bombed, but still very beautiful. The mountainside was studded with temples, each roof a soft curving arabesque against the trees. There were trickling streams and bridges, pilgrims who bought yellow incense sticks or candles of bright scarlet to burn at the hundred holy places. Soft bells tolled at all hours of the day, and many prayers were said to Buddha.

It was in one of the numerous temples that the refugee organization of the Nationalists had been set up. Gladys and the children were given food, and she could sleep at last. Everything was a little dreamlike. So much soft, near tropical beauty was alien to her. Without protest she drank the medicine the children brought to her. Liang and Ninepence insisted that she drink it. She asked them where they had got it from, and they told her from the Buddhist priests. They had told the priests that Ai-weh-deh was ill and demanded medicine from them; the priests provided herbs of various kinds which they must boil in water, and give the liquid to Ai-Weh-Deh when it was cool. It had a bitter taste but was not unpalatable.

She did not really remember how many days they spent in Hua San. She knew only that it had been March when they set out and now it was late in April. Except for the daily quota of cuts and bruises and bumps, and narrow escapes from awful disaster which are the normal hazards of childhood, they were all healthy. The trains ran spasmodically to Sian, and the woman who looked after the refugee center, a keen young Chinese girl imbued with the spirit of the New Life movement which under Madame Chiang Kai-shek's patronage was sweeping China, told her that she must not worry; they would see she got aboard a train for Sian when the time came.

One morning they helped her lead the children down to the railroad station and into the coaches. They gave them food to carry with them, because the journey would take at least three or four days. Chinese trains at that time possessed vagaries beyond the comprehension of the Western mind. They traveled or stopped as the whim took them. Afterward

Gladys could not remember whether the journey took three or four or even five days. The children gamboled, screamed and shouted, as always. The countryside, lovely in the April sunshine, passed slowly before them. They stopped sometimes for hours on end; then they jogged on again through the days and nights. At last, one noontime, she was aware of a communal excitement among all the refugees. She struggled up, and could see the walls and pagodas beyond the station and a jumble of low buildings. The children were already piling out onto the platform, and she realized that she must follow them. Outside the station she assembled them into their familiar column.

"As we march through the gates of Sian we shall sing a hymn," she said.

An old Chinese lifted his head as she spoke.

"Woman," he said, "you will never get into Sian. The gates are closed. No more refugees are allowed into the city."

She did not believe him. She could not believe him. The mute faces of the children were turned up toward her. All these long weeks she had sustained them with the miracle of Sian.

"Where shall we go, then?" she said, desperately. "Where shall we go?"

The old man pointed. "There is a refugee camp near the walls yonder. They will feed you."

It was true. After coming so far, they were shut out. Gladys led the children to the camp and, while the New Life helpers there were feeding them, she walked by herself along the road to the city. As she got closer she could see that the walls were high and buttressed. It was bigger by far than Tsechow. She could see the high, green-tiled roofs of the pagodas above the walls. The massive wooden gates were barred and shut.

The Small Woman

A watcher from the walls above shouted: "Woman! Go away. The city is packed with refugees. No one comes into the city. Woman, go away!"

She leaned her face against the hard surface of the gate and wept. So long a journey! And for this! For this!

CHAPTER SEVENTEEN

SHE WALKED SLOWLY back to rejoin the children, not knowing what to tell them. But they had news for her instead. Representatives of the New Life movement had discovered them. They reaffirmed that it was impossible for them to stay at Sian; for the time being the city was closed to refugees. But it would probably reopen in a few days' time, and in any case, arrangements had been made to care for the children at Fufeng, a near-by city. An orphanage and a school were operating there. All the children Tsin Pen-kuang had brought from Tsechow were already there.

"You mean it's going to be all right? My children will really be cared for?" Gladys asked.

"Yes," they said. "Tomorrow we'll put you on the train to Fufeng. It isn't a long trip."

At first she could hardly believe it. Partly this was because the diseases in her body, the relapsing fever and the typhus, and the internal injuries she was not even aware of, began to take over as soon as the burden of the responsibility was eased. She hardly remembered the train journey to Fufeng, only that there were pleasant young women on the platform, with food, to meet them; smiling girls with armbands of the New Life movement, who marshaled the children and said, "Now, we shall all be happy!"

In Fufeng the children were taken to an old Buddhist temple, given new clothes and shoes, fed, and allotted places to sleep. But Fufeng was hot and humid; and the fever made

248

it all strangely unreal. The children were saved. . . . The long flight was ended. . . . But in the confusion of the fever, she felt as though it were still happening—the mountain peaks, the desolation, the loneliness. Two Chinese women who ran a small Christian mission in Fufeng asked her to go with them to a neighboring village, and preach a sermon. Because she had never concerned herself with her own physical weakness or well-being, she agreed.

But as she walked with the two Chinese women along the sunbaked road, with the green wheat fields stretching away on either side, she found she was having trouble with her feet. They did not seem to want to go down in the right places. When they reached the household she was given a bowl of food and chopsticks and sat on a little stool to eat it. But the food wouldn't go into her mouth; somehow she could not control her hands even to perform such a simple act. It really was most annoying. She wanted the food, yet could not eat it. She noticed the others looking at her rather strangely. Had she a headache? Yes, she had a headache. Would she like to lie down for a little while before she gave her sermon? Yes, she would like to lie down. It must be the heat which made her feel a little odd.

It was nothing, the women said, as they helped her to a small room off the courtyard; she had had a very hard time over the past few weeks and she must be very tired. She must rest for a little while, and in an hour or two she could deliver her sermon.

She stretched out wearily on the hard bed, her Bible by her side. Now, I shall preach from John, she thought. From the woman of Samaria:

Whosoever drinketh of this water shall thirst again. But whosoever drinketh of the water that I shall give him shall

249

never thirst; but the water that I shall give him shall be in him a well of water springing up into everlasting life. . . .

Against her eyeballs she saw a great whirring blaze of color; scarlet and purples and yellows. She felt hot. She tried to raise her hand to her forehead, but it would not lift. No matter . . . the Gospel according to St. John. . . .

Woman, where are those thine accusers? Hath no man condemned thee?

There was a rusty dryness in her throat. If only she could have a little drink. . . . The Gospel according . . .

In the beginning was the Word, and the Word was with God, and the Word was God. The same was in the beginning with God. All things were made by Him. . . . In Him was life; and the life was the light of men. And the light shineth in darkness; and the darkness comprehended it not. . . .

The great lights faded from the back of her eyes and from her brain and she fell downward, downward, into darkness. When they came to fetch her an hour later, she was delirious.

* * * * *

So now the flies were buzzing about the room—a strange room, with a clean bed and a small bedside table, and limp, bright-colored curtains at the windows. Where was she? What had happened? They tried to tell her. She had been brought to Hsing P'ing in an oxcart by some peasants, and to Sian in a private railroad car; she had lain for days and weeks close to death. But now she could not remember thos weeks. And she thought that perhaps, when she was so sick in the strange village home, the Chinese women had become frightened, and had persuaded peasants to take her to the mission in their cart.

There and in Sian, the Senior Physician had taken care of

her, and the nurses, and a great many friends. She wasn't going to die, and she had saved the children. Gradually, while she lay in the hospital bed, all this became clear to her. The children were safe. They had food, and clothes, and even schooling. . . . They had cried when there was no boat to take them across the Yellow River. But now they were safe.

As the days passed, she gradually gained more strength, until presently the Senior Physician was able to arrange for her to be taken out to the house of a friend of his, in the country outside Sian. There, and later in the homes of other friends, they succeeded in nursing her back to some state of health, and she could return to Sian, though she was still not really well.

Linnan came down to visit Sian, and she was glad to see him. He implored her to marry him, and go with him to Chungking, where he was now stationed. But somehow, away from the mountain country, here in Sian, their relationship had altered. She did not know what it was, only that things were different. She knew that if the war had not driven her out of Shansi, she would have married Linnan, and her life would have taken quite another course.

"Wait," she had said then. "We cannot get married while this terrible war is on, or while we are here fighting." He had waited, and it was too late. Now, instead of that inner exultation, the rounded delight of knowing that she loved and was loved in return, there was this nagging anxiety to do the right thing by her God, her children, and the man she loved.

Somewhere in the mountains between Yangcheng and the Yellow River, somewhere on the plains between the Yellow River and the old capital of Sian, somewhere in the unreal world of delirium and the fevers of her illness, certitude had

251

been replaced by anxiety. All this, in tears, she tried to tell Linnan; all this in the despair of his love he tried to brush aside, and say that it would be better when she was well. In Chungking, he said, he would have high rank; they could make a home there and be happy; the children could go to school there. But it was no use; the colored bird had flown away. Perhaps it could not live in the forest of deep despair that grew all over China. There was so much work to be done for the Lord, and she, the small woman, the small disciple, had her part to play in that work.

She said good-by to him at the station outside Sian, and walked back through the narrow streets with an overwhelming ache of loneliness in her heart, aware that she would never know completely if she had acted wisely or not—only that through all her waking days she would remember Linnan as the one man she had loved. The war swept him away and she never saw him again.

As her health gradually improved, the Small Woman continued her work, in China, and later in England. She worked for the New Life movement in Sian and started a Christian church for refugees in the city. Then she settled at Paochi, farther westward in Shensi province, and later took a job with an American Methodist mission in Szechwan, near the borders of Tibet, and worked among the lepers there. She kept her five children with her, and gave them a home and an education. They went away to school, Ninepence got married, and Gladys was left alone. She had sent them out into the world.

But although she was able to carry on her work, she still had to struggle against impaired health. When the Japanese had beaten her up in the courtyard that day at Tsechow, they had inflicted severe internal injuries which grew more serious as the years passed. The European doctors she consulted told her that her only chance was to return to England and be operated upon there. But since she had no money, that was impossible; her chief hope was that some day she could return to her beloved Yangcheng.

Some time after leaving Paochi she went up to Tzechung to hand over one of the Methodist missions to a group of Americans who had been driven out of northern Shansi and had come to the West to continue their work. She was chatting with one of them as they walked along the road to the mission, when they passed a refugee woman from Shansi whom Gladys knew slightly. The woman hailed her in the Shansi dialect and Gladys replied in the same idiom. The American looked down at her with interest.

"You've been in that part of China?" he asked.

"Yes," said Gladys. "I was up in Shansi."

"I don't suppose," he said, "you've happened to hear about that woman missionary called Ai-weh-deh who ran around behind the Japanese lines years ago? Never met her, did you? She must have been quite a gal. Certainly left some stories behind her."

"Yes, I knew her," said Gladys quietly. "That was me."

The American looked astonished. "Well, I'll be darned," he said. "I'm honored!"

They talked for a long time and he asked when she had last been home. She didn't understand what he meant.

"Back to England," he said.

She smiled. "What chance have I of going back to England when I hardly know where tomorrow's dinner is coming from?"

His eyes widened. "How long have you been here?"

"Seventeen years!"

"And no leave in all that time?" he said. "But you'd like to go home, wouldn't you?"

"It would be nice to see them all again, I suppose," she said wistfully, "but it's quite impossible." The conversation changed. She forgot all about it, even if the American did not. A few weeks later he rejoined his wife in Shanghai. She had been administering a fund raised in the United States to repatriate German Protestant missionaries and orphans. Many of them, good, stouthearted people, had been close to starvation, but now all the repatriations were completed, and a few hundred dollars still remained in the fund. Later on, the wife of the American told Gladys how it happened when they met in Shanghai.

He had approached his wife very seriously. "Listen, dear," he had said. "I've found something very useful for you to do with those dollars you've got left."

"Well?" she said.

"This is not for an orphan, and not for a German. This is for a little woman, a little Englishwoman named Gladys Aylward. I think it would be kind of nice if you used that money to send her home for a trip. She's in bad health. I've found out that much from her friends. Now, let me tell you a little about her. . . ."

The first that Gladys Aylward knew about this typical act of American generosity was when one of the Chinese Elders, a cheerful, friendly old man, came up to the village in the mountains where she was staying. He jogged down the village street and, seeing her standing at the Mission door, waved a letter at her and shouted, "I've been sent to find you. You're going back to England."

She looked at him in a bewildered way. "What are you talking about?" she said.

His face was one wide grin. "All you have to do is to go to

Shanghai, and your fare will be paid to England. You're going home. Now what are you crying about, woman? Isn't that news good enough for you?"

Only after long further consideration did Gladys Aylward decide that God wished her to return to England, and therefore she should go. So it was that the Small Woman, some years after the war, returned to her native land so that she could have medical treatment to correct some of the injuries resulting from the brutalities of the Japanese at Tsechow.

Since leaving the hospital where she was operated upon, Gladys Aylward has traveled throughout England, lecturing and preaching at churches and schools and mission halls. She has been a second mother to scores of Chinese students from Singapore and Hong Kong arriving in England to study. She has played a large part in helping to set up a hostel in Liverpool for Chinese seamen and other Chinese nationals. As always, she has lived frugally and simply, and from day to day.

Probably Gladys Aylward will always be plagued by ill health because of what she experienced in China. But she will carry with her something else, too—the memory of a hundred singing children, and a broad swirling river, and prayers that were answered, and strangers who were kind. Year after year, she hears from those children, grown now into men and women, but still bound by ties of love to their mother, Ai-weh-deh.

Gladys Aylward is shy, and very modest. She carries these things in her heart; she rarely speaks of them. A little parlor-maid from London traveled alone across Siberia, because of a single letter from a woman she had never met. . . . A young girl lived alone for years in a remote mountain city, speaking a strange language, wearing native clothes, becoming friend and counselor to a people so foreign in thought and culture that at first their every custom must have seemed alien. A single-minded and determined girl conversed for hours with a learned Mandarin as he propounded the intricate subtleties of his philosophy. Yet, armed only with her own forthright experience and inspired intuitions, she converted him finally to Christianity. A woman, tireless and fearless, traveled alone, month after month, through the dangerous mountain regions of Shansi, on errands of mercy, and errands of war.

This woman was Gladys Aylward, Ai-weh-deh, the Virtuous One. They will not forget her in Shansi. And those who have known her since will not forget her either. For Gladys Aylward is one of the remarkable women of our generation, possessing an inner exaltation, and an abiding tenacity of purpose, that can make anything possible. Even a trip across the wild and pitiless mountains of China, without money, without food, and with a hundred children.

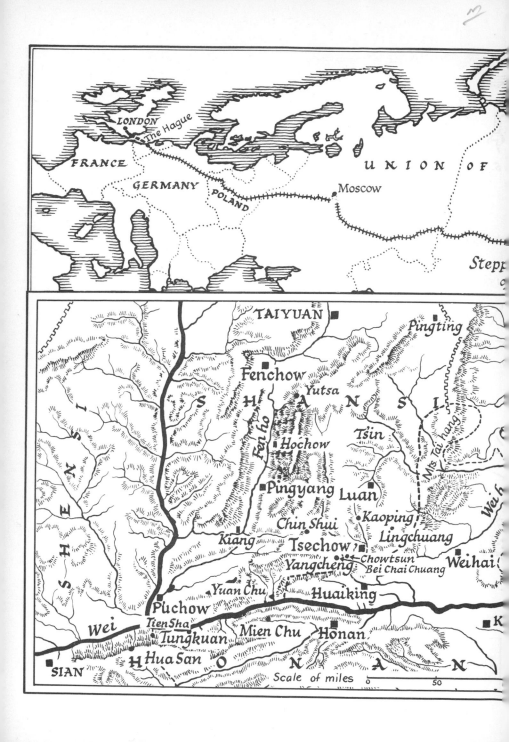

Upper map (labels):

LONDON
The Hague
FRANCE
GERMANY
POLAND
Moscow
U N I O N   O F
Stepp

Lower map (labels):

TAIYUAN
Pingting
Fenchow
Yutsa
S H A N S I
Fen ho
Hochow
Ts'in
Pingyang
Luan
Chin Shui
Kaoping
Kiang
Lingchuang
Tsechow
Yangcheng
Chowtsun
Bei Chai Chuang
Weihai
Yuan Chu
Huaiking
Puchow
Wei
Tien Sha
Tungkuan
Mien Chu
Honan
Hua San
H O N A N
SIAN
S H E N S I
Wei h
K

Scale of miles   0   50